ARTBARN

ARTBARN

The Stern Collection

Dedicated with love to Jerome and Ellen Stern

Jerome Stern in front of Liu Wei
Landscape - Celestial Mountain

CONTENTS

Foreword

by Lynda Stern

When I first approached my father Jerry with a mock-up of the ArtBarn book, I thought he would be elated. The project had been in the works for months, and everything had been photographed secretly—requiring great coordination to keep him from running into the photographers while they were on site. There were quite a few close calls.

Instead, surprising us all with a very out of character response, he was upset—angry, even—at the idea of a book being published on his collection.

He had lovingly curated hundreds, if not thousands, of pieces over more than sixty years, not for the recognition, but out of a sense of appreciation and eclectic personal taste. He saw the beauty, wit, and distinctiveness in works that others may have overlooked. He was an early collector of many unknown and burgeoning artists who often became dear friends.

That was the spirit and legacy I wanted to capture in the publication, but he felt the collection was not worthy of a book, that he was not a "real" collector of the same caliber as some of his contemporaries who had amassed high-profile collections with even more legendary artists. He approached his collection, and the ArtBarn itself, with a humility that at first made him resistant to the book.

Fortunately, he eventually came around. He even became an active participant in the project, sending over articles and photos of how other collections were documented. He came to understand that having a physical record of the ArtBarn's collection could be not only of interest to others but an enduring and inspiring gift.

Jerry was kind, generous, and funny. He was curious, open to the world. He remained an intrepid traveler well into his late eighties. He was a family man who maintained close relationships with each and every member of his big family, down to the great-grandchildren. His greatest pleasure was sharing his joy, whether through art, storytelling, or hosting friends and family. He loved giving tours of the ArtBarn, delighted in walking his visitors through the moments of hidden humor that he had so thoughtfully curated.

Now, with this book, Jerry's unique artistic sensibility and hundreds of the incredible works he collected are preserved and showcased for the first time, both for those who loved Jerry and the ArtBarn, and all who now have the privilege to be introduced to his legacy.

Introduction

A CONTEMPORARY WUNDERKAMMER

by Christopher Phillips

Among the many mesmerizing works on view at the ArtBarn—the Westhampton exhibition space that once housed contemporary art from the sprawling Stern collection—was Mark Dion's *The Great Chain of Being* (1979; page 17, 85). A massive wooden cabinet whose shelves are crowded with botanical and zoological specimens, bones, and tiny objets d'art, Dion's work is meant to evoke a Wunderkammer, one of those "cabinets of curiosities" that are among the early precursors of today's museum collections. Any precise relations among these assorted, enigmatic objects are left for the visitor to tease out by means of careful visual comparisons and imaginative leaps. Seen in the context of the ArtBarn, Dion's cabinet served as an emblem for the remarkable ensemble of works that filled the building and surrounding grounds.

Stern's ArtBarn was a rare venture. Although it has been referred to as a private museum, the ArtBarn was far more informal and idiosyncratic than that. Simply locating it required a bit of detective work. Searching for a website or even a phone number yielded nothing. Those who discovered a connection, through a family friend or an artist, for example, could make an appointment to visit the Sterns' eighteen-acre, waterfront estate in Westhampton. There, just a short walk from the main residence, they would find not a barn but a spacious industrial-style facility set among verdant trees.

For all its boxy structural efficiency, the ArtBarn was a highly personal showplace filled with works acquired by an eager, committed collector for both his own satisfaction and the enjoyment of his guests. It is common for individuals who prospered in business, as Jerome Stern did in the world of venture capital and finance, to become fascinated by the realm of art and artists. However, in the ArtBarn, an uncommon set of rules applied and the imaginative side of life was given freer rein. Having begun to collect in the mid-1960s, Stern came to understand, through a deep engagement and his own independent temperament, the unpredictable pleasures of art more thoroughly than many museum professionals. He developed an informed yet unconventional point of view about modern and contemporary art, and a clear sense of what pleased him about it. Merely beautiful works lost their appeal early on, and abstraction for its own sake never appeared to have exercised a strong pull.

Judging by certain paintings and sculptures that entered the Stern collection in the early years, one might speculate that Stern's predilection for Surrealist works by Max Ernst, Victor Brauner, and Joseph Cornell was crucial to pinpointing his subsequent interests in contemporary art. Those interests center on the human figure, its surrogates and its transformations; on the mysteries of everyday objects and materials and their unexpected associations; and on leavening the seriousness of art with jolts of erotica and outright humor. Among the many works in the ArtBarn that exhibit these qualities are Hans Breder's black-and-white photographs from his *Body/Sculpture* series of 1969–73 (page 134). The four prints show a nude young woman in dizzyingly contorted postures, often accompanied by mirrors that multiply her twisting limbs. Breder's model was his then-student Ana Mendieta, later a significant artist in her own right, whose calmly grotesque facial distortions were also displayed at the ArtBarn in her 1972 images from *Untitled (Glass on Body Imprints)* (page 48).

Not surprisingly then, Stern was evidently drawn to artists and artworks that determinedly, gleefully flouted the art world's rules and shattered its decorum. Although most of the more-than-200 works gathered in the ArtBarn might initially be categorized as portraits, figure studies, still lifes, or landscapes, almost every piece on view ultimately upends those familiar rubrics. The ArtBarn was conceived not long after Stern acquired *Empty Dream* (1995; below, page 38), a nine-by-twenty-four–foot photo-work by Mariko Mori. In this multi-panel panorama, the Japanese artist appears as a languidly glamorous mermaid stretched out on the sand of an artificial indoor beach. Realizing that he had no space to accommodate the work in his Long Island house or his Manhattan

apartment—both were already brimming with art—Stern turned to Serge Spitzer, a Romanian-born, New York-based artist and trusted friend whom he had known since the early 1980s. Stern commissioned Spitzer to design an exhibition space on the grounds of the estate. Completed in 2000, the ArtBarn (so-named by Stern to underscore his disregard for grandeur) then became the living heart of the growing Stern collection. The roughly 10,000 square foot building had well-proportioned gallery spaces on two levels, as well as a catwalk running the length of one wall where additional works were displayed. An open storage and staging room allowed visitors to examine works that had recently arrived or were about to be sent out as loans to museum exhibitions, shipping crates often strewn amongst the artworks.

After spending some time amid the sculptures, paintings, drawings, photographs, and installations in the ArtBarn's galleries, one realized that they had been placed in apparently neutral but in fact slyly calculated groupings. Recognizable works by celebrated artists—among them Yayoi Kusama, Joseph Beuys, Michelangelo Pistoletto, Yinka Shonibare, John Coplans, and Wolfgang Laib— shared the stage with equally impressive works created by artists whose names were much less familiar. These names usually proved to be the ones known to the most adventurous, curious, and peripatetic collectors and curators. It was also evident that the ArtBarn welcomed contemporary art from every corner of the globe, not only Europe and North America but Africa, Latin America, Asia, and the Middle East as well. This was not trendy or token internationalism but the expression of a collector's sure instincts. Non-Western artists were held in a dialogue of equals with their Western counterparts. Works by Liu Wei, Huang Yong Ping, Zhang Huan, Zheng Guogu, and Wang Jin—only a few of whom enjoy wide recognition in this country—entered into the sophisticated ricochet of images and ideas that was the most distinctive feature of the ArtBarn display.

Indeed, a fast and furious interplay was set in motion by the selection and placement of art throughout the space. Some pieces engaged in a witty game of reference to well-known works, styles, and movements of the past. Take Liu Wei's imposing, mural-scale *Landscape - Celestial Mountain* from 2004 (page 60), which appears to be an oversize classical Chinese ink painting when seen from a distance. Closer inspection reveals it to be a gelatin silver photograph in five parts, and the pictured "mountain" to be an irreverent arrangement of nude bodies, bent over and bums-up. Sabrina Mezzaqui's 2004 *The Arabian Nights* (page 74), a hanging sculpture made from rolled-up pages of the classic tales, over two hundred feet long in full, descended in modular segments from the gallery rafters to coil into a circle on the floor. The work suggested an inverted version of Brancusi's *Endless Column* (1938), the segments of which rose into the infinity of the sky. And Sylvie Fleury's *Slim-Fast* (1993; below left, page 181), a group of eight wooden blocks screen printed to resemble cartons of the popular diet drink, paid winking homage to Andy Warhol's plywood "Brillo Boxes" of the 1960s. The Italian duo Bertozzi & Casoni took on the Pop master directly with the trompe-l'oeil *Brillo Box* (2005; below right, page 108)—soiled and open to show the trash within—made entirely of glazed ceramic.

Along with serving up suggestive references to the art of the past, the works gathered in the ArtBarn also engaged in lively repartee with one another. The gray felt suit by Joseph Beuys, which hung so respectably from a clothes hanger on the gallery wall, paired up with the woman's dress, equipped with jarringly lifelike replicas of hands and feet, installed on a hanger and almost concealed within Paloma Varga Weisz's barrel-like wooden sculpture, *Cabinet* (2008; page 92). The three tall, vaselike sculptures of Huang Yong Ping's *Wells* (2007; page 80), each containing a taxidermy animal gazing up to meet the eyes of the startled viewer, found an unlikely counterpart in the hollowed stones of Wang Jin's outdoor *Installation People's Republic*

of China (2004; page 2, 283). Bending down to peer into the core of each stone, the viewer encountered the imploring face of a tiny human figure.

A more caustic kind of interplay between the ArtBarn works was triggered by the striking similarity between the fields of white dots that fill Thomas Ruff's large photo work *55 Degrees* (1990; page 64), a monumental C-print, and Bai Yiluo's enormous *Flies II* (2001; page 251), an equally imposing photogram. The starry sky in Ruff's astronomical image announces the majesty of the universe. That cosmic vision is brought crashing down to earth in the work of Chinese artist Yiluo, who employed a mundane and frankly repellant material to create his unique dot pattern: the collected remains of thousands of dead flies.

When one spent time with the works in the ArtBarn, an entire network of eccentric "family relations" came into view, affiliating the pieces in multiple, satisfying ways. An awkward, spindly-legged motif, for example, linked a wide range of sculptures, from Huang Yong Ping's *Chapeau à huit pattes (Eight-Legged Hat)* (2000; page 88), to Kim Jones's *Untitled (Doll)* (2004–11; left, page 194), and Wangechi Mutu's *Blackthrone VIII* (2012; page 31). Variations on the concept of "chair"—that everyday meeting-point of the human body and materialized form—emerged as a common thread that ran from Mutu's works to Doris Salcedo's wooden chair embedded in a heavy concrete block (page 55), Axel Lieber's miniature *Short Cuts* (2005; page 193), and an alarmingly distressed sling chair by Edward Kienholz (below, page 235). Related, if more practical, was the outdoor bench designed by Scott Burton (page 277).

From the outset, a defining aspect of the presentation in the ArtBarn was the creation of a dialogue between two mediums that are seldom considered in tandem: contemporary sculpture and photography. As it turns out, some of the most adventurous photographic work of recent decades could be described as explorations of sculptural ideas by other means. John Coplans's tightly framed photographs of his own hands and interlocking fingers

(page 42), for example, suggest the formal power of primitivist sculptures. An echoing work by Dieter Appelt consists of unnerving photographs of the artist's bandaged, archaic-looking hands: the grimy aftermath of a performance in which he attempted to purge himself of his memories of encountering decaying bodies during World War II (page 250).

A more casual, improvisational interpretation of sculptural ideas could be seen in Erwin Wurm's *Untitled (Red Sweaters/One Minute Sculptures)* (2000; page 216). In this grid of fifty color photographs of an ordinary red sweater in a pristine white studio, a commonplace item of apparel is off-handedly transformed into a series of mock-sculptural forms. Equally quixotic is the large five-panel photo work *Prinzip Hoffnung (Potato Peel)* (1986–87; page 56) by Anna and Bernhard Blume, in which curling strips of potato peels, dramatically lit and photographed in close-up, become bold sculptural objects that display swirling, calligraphic forms.

Other works at the ArtBarn turned the photographic print itself into a kind of sculptural object. A nearly complete transformation of photographs into three-dimensional objects takes place in Katrín Sigurdardóttir's untitled sculptural work of 2006 (below, page 240). The artist has used small aerial photographs of Iceland's capital, Reykjavik, as a surface upon which she fashions polystyrene reliefs. Set in small, nested wooden boxes that are placed on the floor, the reliefs suggest fragmented, three-dimensional urban topographies. Carlos Garaicoa's untitled work of 2003 is part of a series of large black-and-white photographs that show undistinguished urban settings in Havana and its environs (page 226). By meticulously pinning lengths of colored thread to the prints, Garaicoa ingeniously conjures up the outlines of towering modern buildings: a phantom architecture that anticipates the changes that lie in store for twenty first-century Cuba. This work also subtly resonates with an untitled Fred Sandback piece from 1987 that employed three strands of tautly stretched red and white yarn to define a geometric form in a corner of the adjacent ArtBarn gallery (page 246).

More than a dozen outdoor sculptures and installations were sited around the Stern property, and they contributed their own considerable share of inventiveness, impudence, and striking presence to the natural setting. Visitors encountered a regally scaled yet roughly carved wood figure by Stephan Balkenhol (page 264). The seven-foot-tall man, wearing everyday clothes and unremarkable but for the chalk-white hands that match his shirt, gazed across the land, wide-eyed but impassive. Visitors may have been startled to come upon a bronze fountain by Ann-Sofi Sidén that depicts the artist squatting, eyes closed, and relieving herself (page 260). As if to acknowledge that men, too, must answer the call of nature, there was a counterpart work by David Hammons, a white ceramic urinal incongruously strapped to a tree (page 259).

A contemporary Wunderkammer, the ArtBarn embraced a collection of seemingly disparate works that finally revealed themselves to be part of a web of unanticipated artistic linkages. Where else could one find in close proximity Frederick Kiesler's *Galaxy A* (1961; page 208), a whirl of freeform drawings and blocky wooden forms; Wolfgang Laib's *Milkstone* (1992–95; page 210), whose milk-covered marble surface appears to be at once solid and liquid; and Nobuyoshi Araki's photograph of a young woman whose skin is crisscrossed by the faint traces of a rope bondage session (page 133)? The ArtBarn was a stunning tribute to Stern's practiced eye and to the generous, inclusive, and endlessly connective spirit that he brought to the art of collecting.

ON JEROME STERN AND THE ARTBARN

by Lisa Phillips

I recall the first time I went to the ArtBarn, back when it was still under construction in 2000. Serge Spitzer, the international artist and the architect of the ArtBarn, was with us. I had recently joined the New Museum as its second director, and I was getting to know the collector Jerome Stern—Jerry—who would later join our board. Private museums started by contemporary art collectors were beginning to sprout up everywhere, but the ArtBarn was unusual: the building had been designed from the ground up by an artist. I was bowled over when I saw it—not only by its clarity and beauty, but by its industrial ethos. All the materials were inexpensive, mass-produced, and readily available. They had used only standard, off-the-shelf materials, just reorienting them slightly to produce a new effect. The structure was simple and functional.

My experience that day of this straightforward, lucid space for art helped give me the confidence and determination to build the New Museum's first free-standing home. If Jerry could do it, we also could build something vastly more beautiful—and functional—than our current quarters in a commercial loft space on Broadway, and do it at a cost we could afford. We didn't need starchitects (though our architects did become widely known and admired after our building was completed). Good architecture could be built for a reasonable cost, and we didn't need fancy materials that would only distract from the art on view. The ArtBarn was basic, tough, efficient, and elegant—exactly the qualities that we sought.

Serge was more than the architect of the ArtBarn. He was a close friend of Jerry's, and they really were collaborators on the building and on the collection it housed. They spent a lot of time together, looking at art and talking about it. Both men took great pleasure in what they accomplished together, and they loved to share it with friends and colleagues. The staff and supporters of the New Museum took numerous trips to Quiogue to visit the ArtBarn and keep up with its rotating selection of new art and outdoor commissions situated on the peaceful grounds amid native woods, specimen trees, and wetlands. Jerry and Ellen, his wife, always warmly welcomed their guests with food, drink, and the company of their family and friends.

Jerry, as mentioned, became a trustee of the New Museum, and together with Ellen travelled extensively with us, often adding works to the Stern collection as we visited artists' studios and galleries around the world. Jerry's enthusiasm for art and curiosity about the new was utterly amazing and inspiring. Often, he would have more energy and stamina than the curators and I combined. We had to keep an eye on him, though, because sometimes his curiosity would take him off course. Once, in Mexico City, we lost him for an hour. Thank goodness for cell phones!

When our own new building on the Bowery opened in 2007, Ellen and Jerry were there. They had supported the project generously, and we named our beautiful restrooms for them—by their choice. This truly encapsulates Jerry's understanding of functionality and of the areas in a museum that are genuinely useful to the staff and the public alike. Choosing the restrooms to bear your name clearly was not about ego or pride or social cachet. This was a maverick gesture, akin to the naming of the Jay Chiat loading dock and the Phil and Shelley Aarons staff lounge: acknowledgments of practical support for the unglamorous but essential behind-the-scenes aspects of presenting and enjoying art.

Jerry was a special individual, and he was a true inspiration to us and to all who experienced his joyful and independent spirit that was so beautifully reflected in the ArtBarn.

MAIN
GALLERY

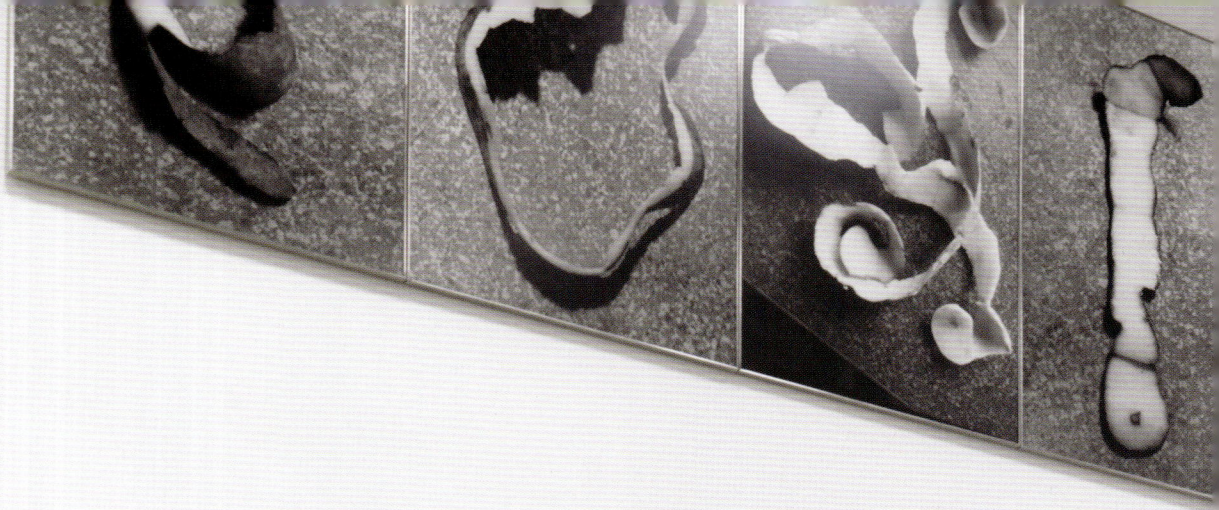

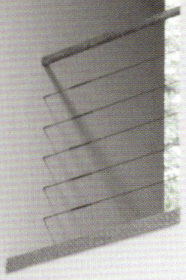

FACING PAGE

Ulrich Rückriem
Zwischen Tür und Angel I
(Between Door and Hinge)
1998
Swedish granite, in four parts
157⅛ × 39⅓ × 31½ in. (400.1 × 99.9 × 80 cm)

ABOVE

Wangechi Mutu
Blackthrone VIII
2012
Wooden chair, plastic, hair, tinsel
100⅞ × 26⅞ × 39⅞ in. (256.2 × 68.3 × 101.3 cm)

ABOVE

Yayoi Kusama
Accumulation on Cabinet No. 1
1963
Stuffed sewn fabric, wooden cabinet,
chicken wire, paint, various objects
60 ½ × 42 ½ × 17 ½ in. (153.7 × 108 ×
44.5 cm)

FACING PAGE

Yayoi Kusama
Untitled (Mannequin)
1966
Mannequin, wig, shoes, paint
58 ⅛ × 25 ½ × 16 in. (148.6 × 64.8 × 40.6 cm)

Joseph Beuys

Felt Suit
1970
Raw felt, sewn, stamped
27½ × 39 in. (69.9 × 99.1 cm)

Das Schweigen (The Silence)
1973
Five reels of Ingmar Bergman's *The Silence* (1963), galvanized, dipped in ink
1⅝ × 15 in. (4.1 × 38.1 cm)

Schlitten (Sled)
1969
Wooden sled, felt, belts, flashlight, fat, rope
13¾ × 35½ × 13¾ in. (34.9 × 90.2 × 34.9 cm)

Wangechi Mutu

Second Born
2013
Collagraph, relief, digital printing, collage, hand coloring
36 × 43 in. (91.4 × 109.2 cm)

Wangechi Mutu
My Strength Lies (Diptych)
2006
Ink, acrylic, photo collage, contact paper
on Mylar
Each 98 × 53 in. (248.9 × 134.6 cm)

Mariko Mori

Empty Dream

1995

C-print, wood, smoked aluminum, six elements

Each 108 × 48 × 3 in. (274.3 × 121.9 × 7.6 cm)

John Coplans
Frieze No. 4, Three Panels, 1994
1994
Nine gelatin silver prints
Each set of three 78 × 34 × 3 in. (198.1 × 86.4 × 7.6 cm)

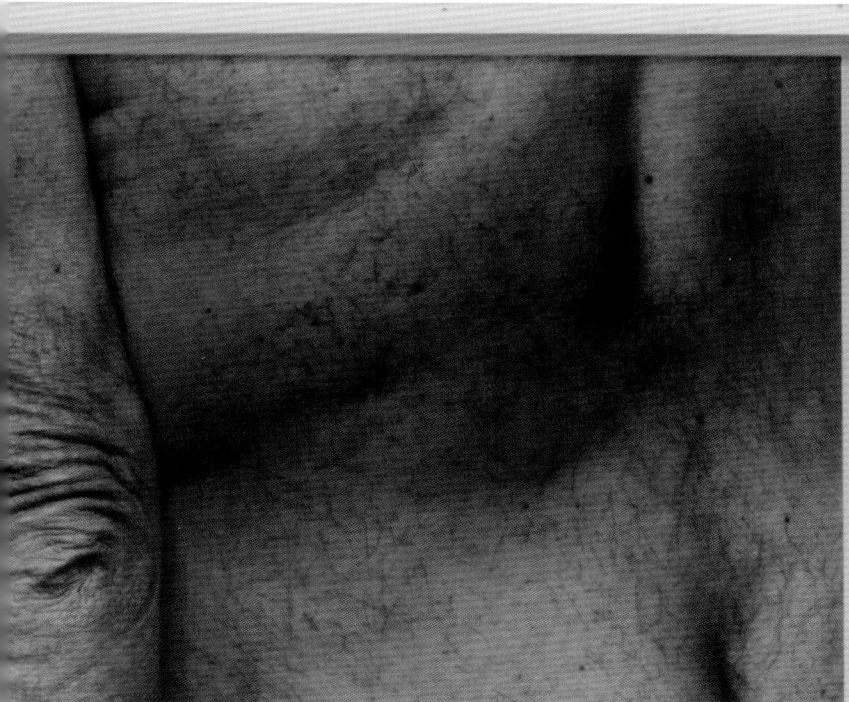
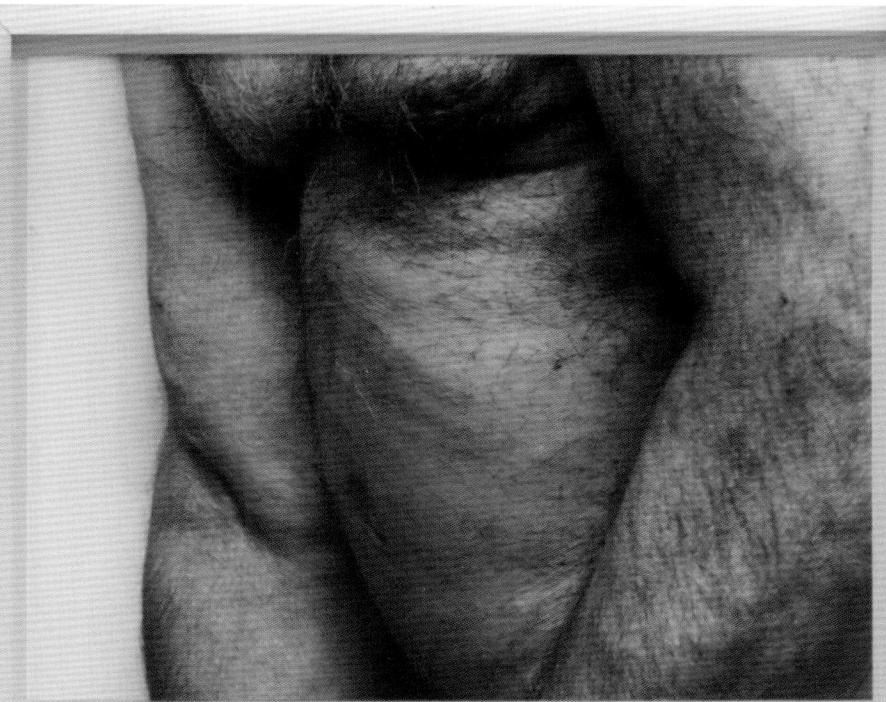
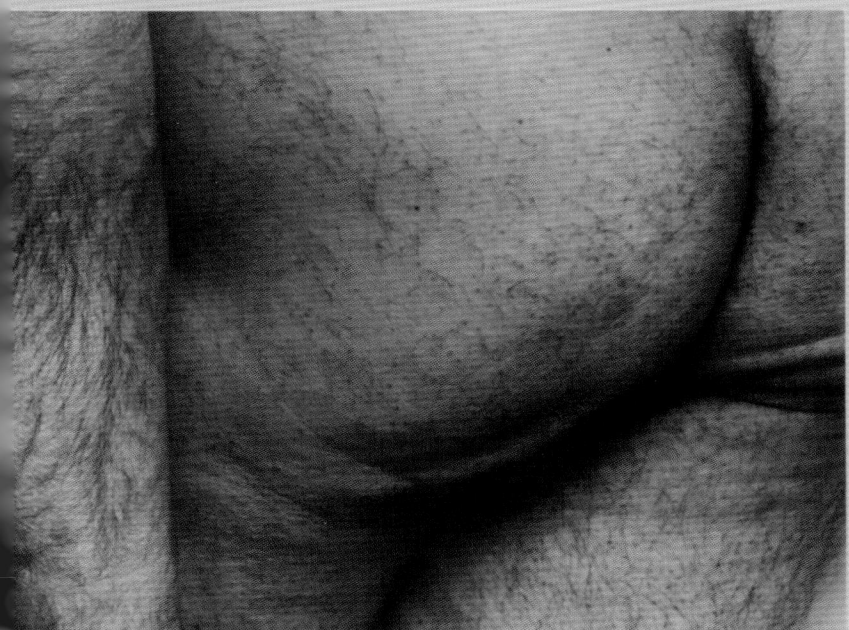
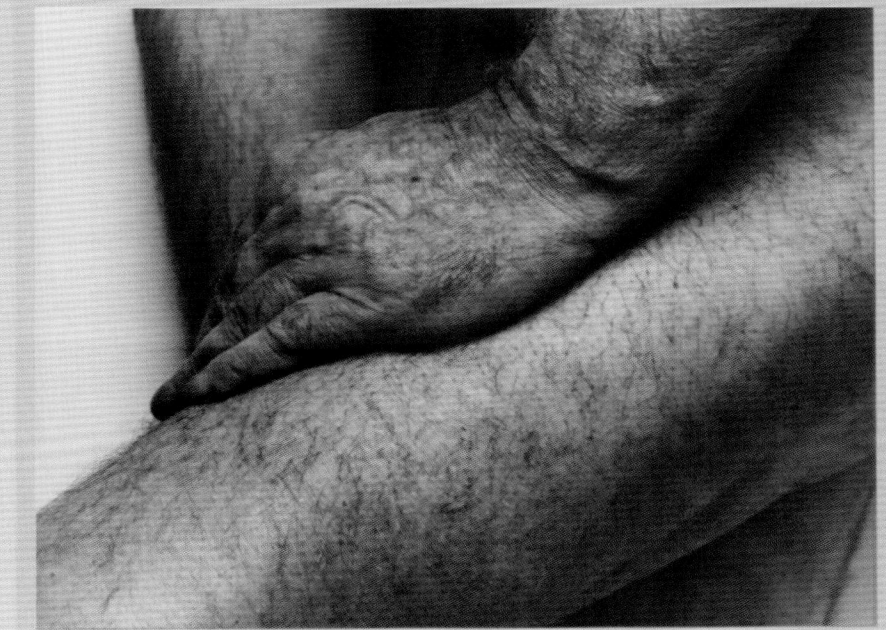
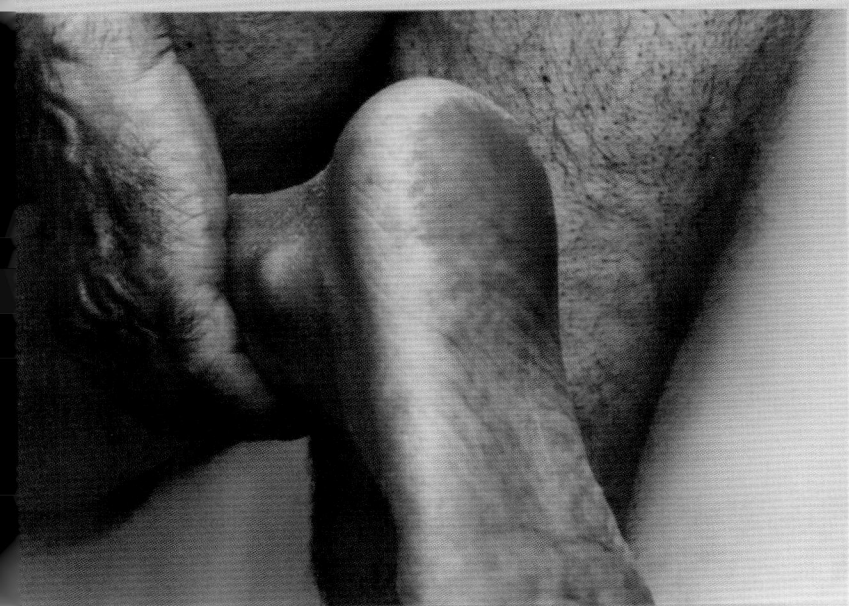
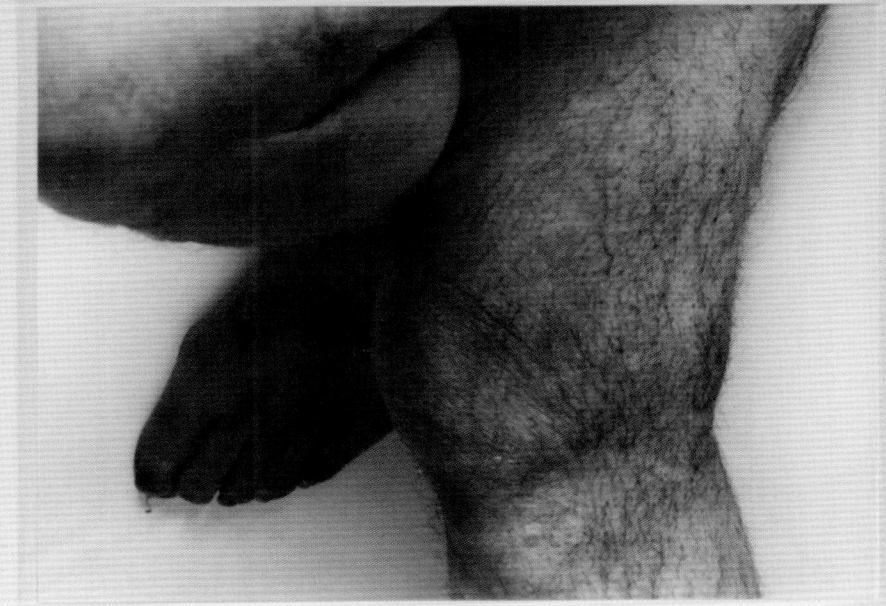

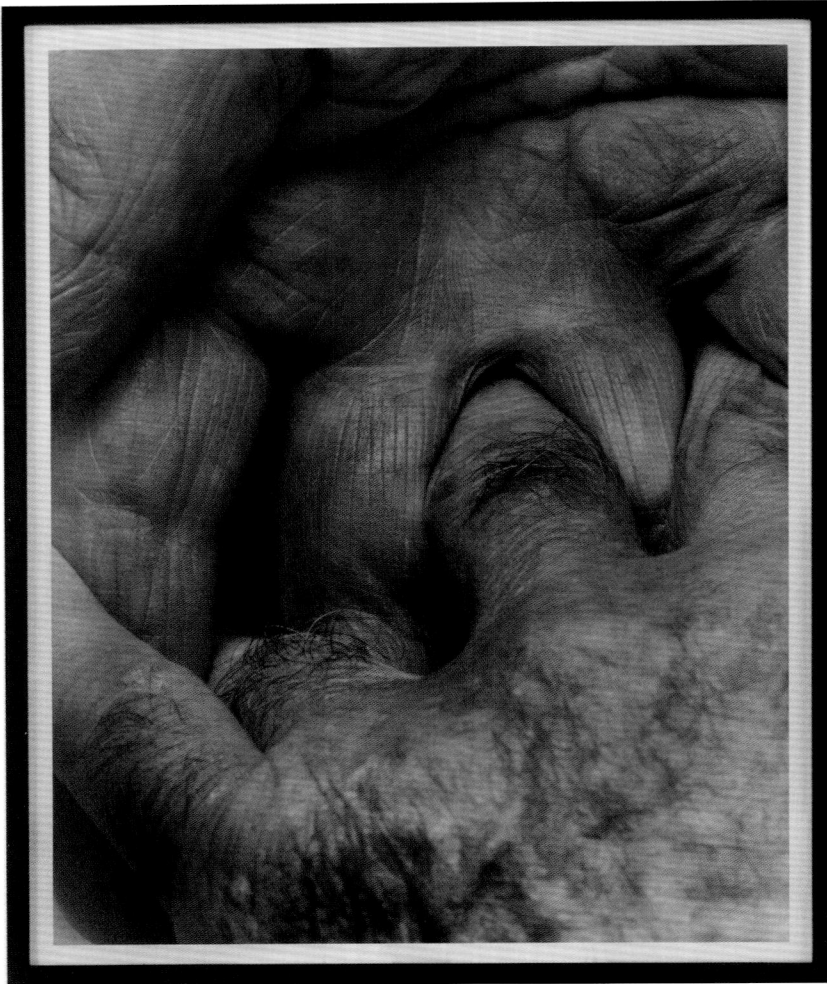

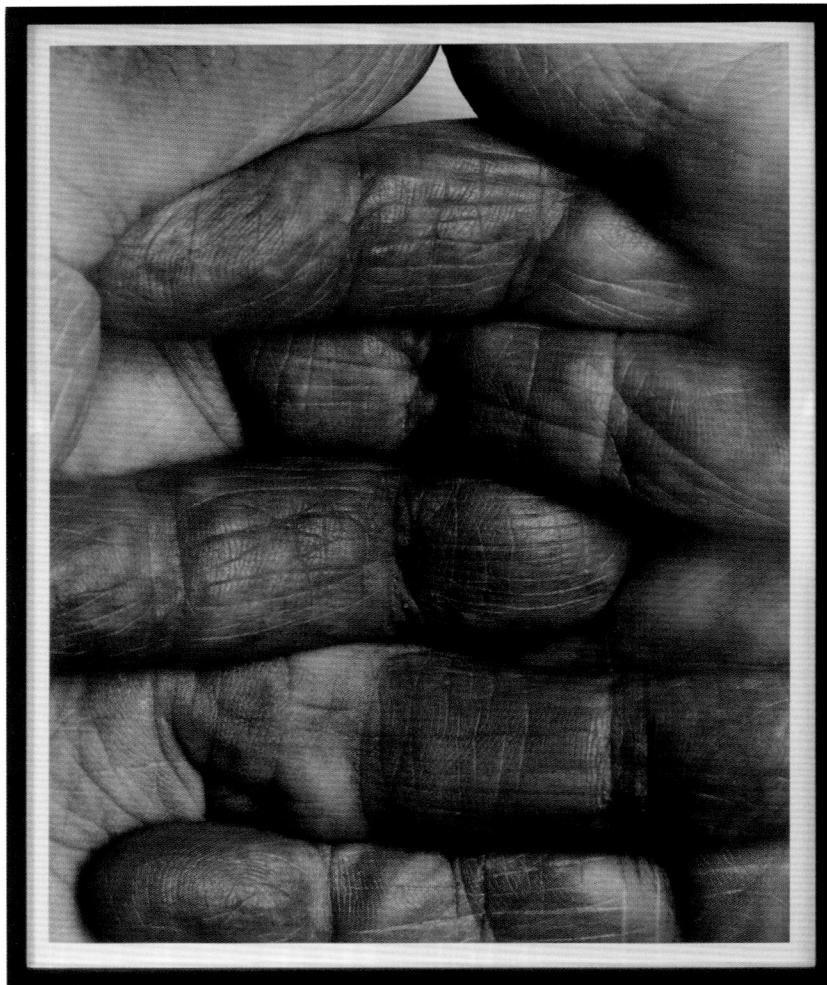

LEFT

John Coplans
Interlocking Fingers No. 2, 1999
1999
Gelatin silver print
35½ × 28⅝ in. (90.2 × 72.7 cm)

Interlocking Fingers No. 1, 1999
1999
Gelatin silver print
35½ × 28⅝ in. (90.2 × 72.7 cm)

FACING PAGE

Zhang Huan
Family Tree
2000
Nine C-prints
Each 21⅛ × 16½ in. (53.7 × 41.9 cm)

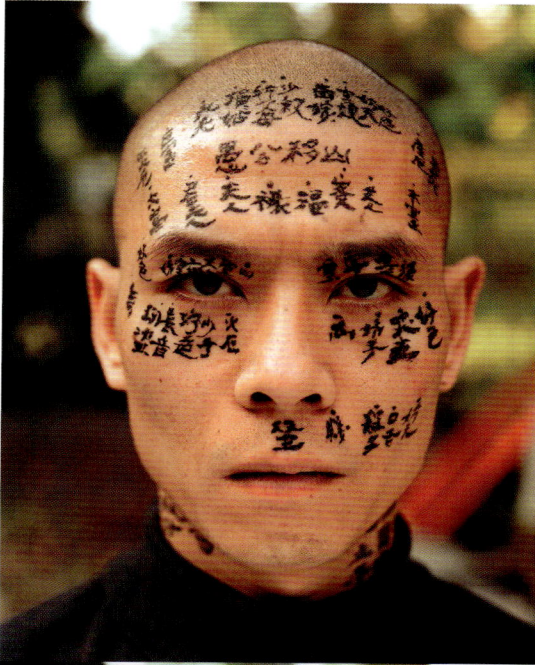
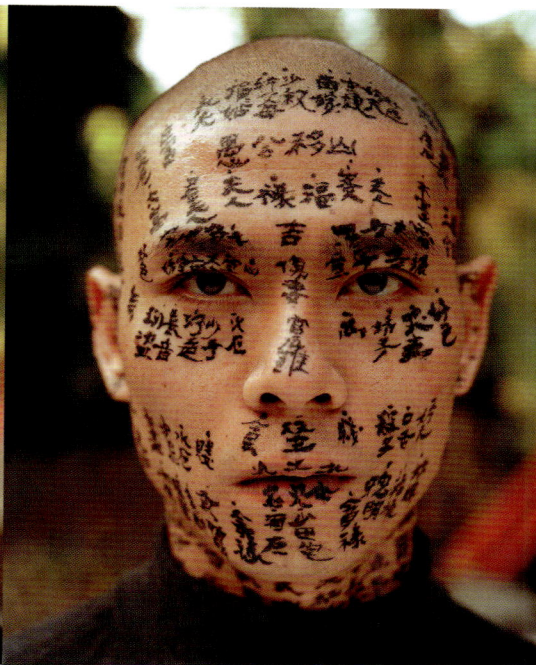
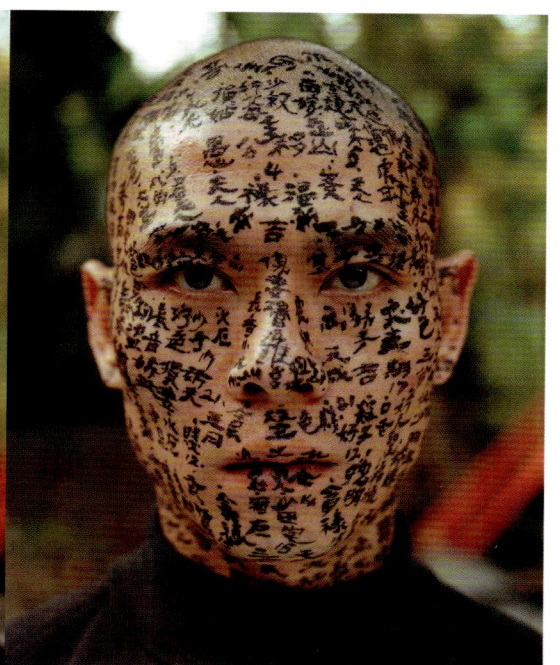
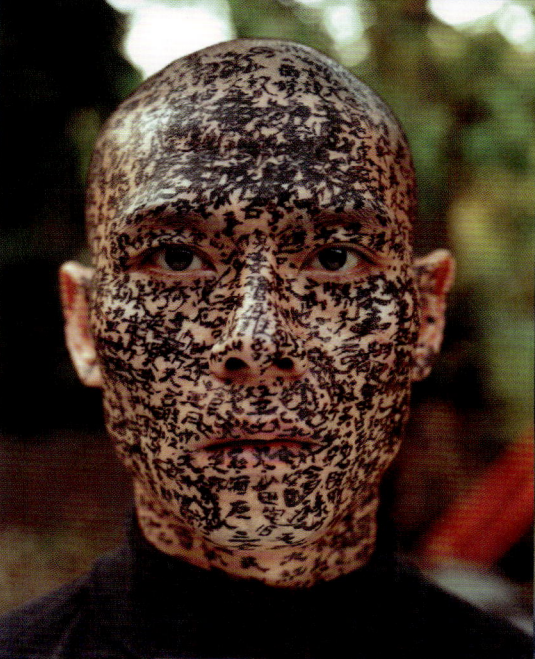
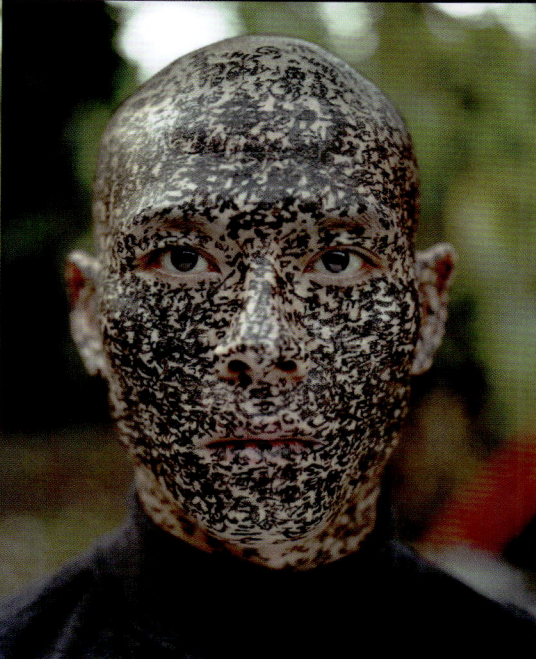
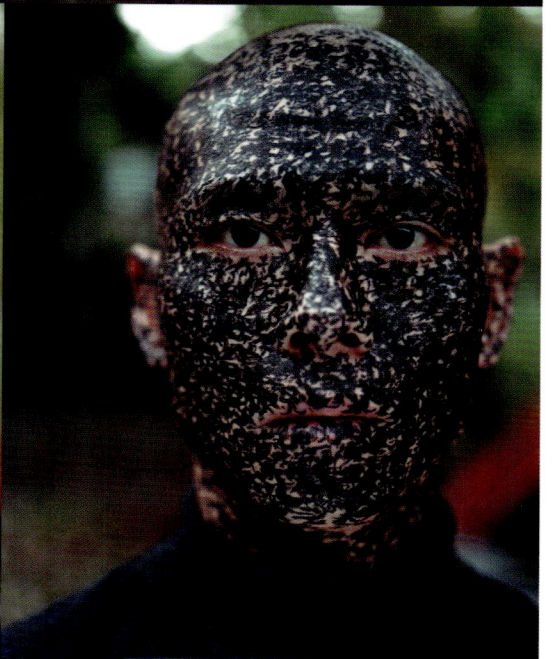

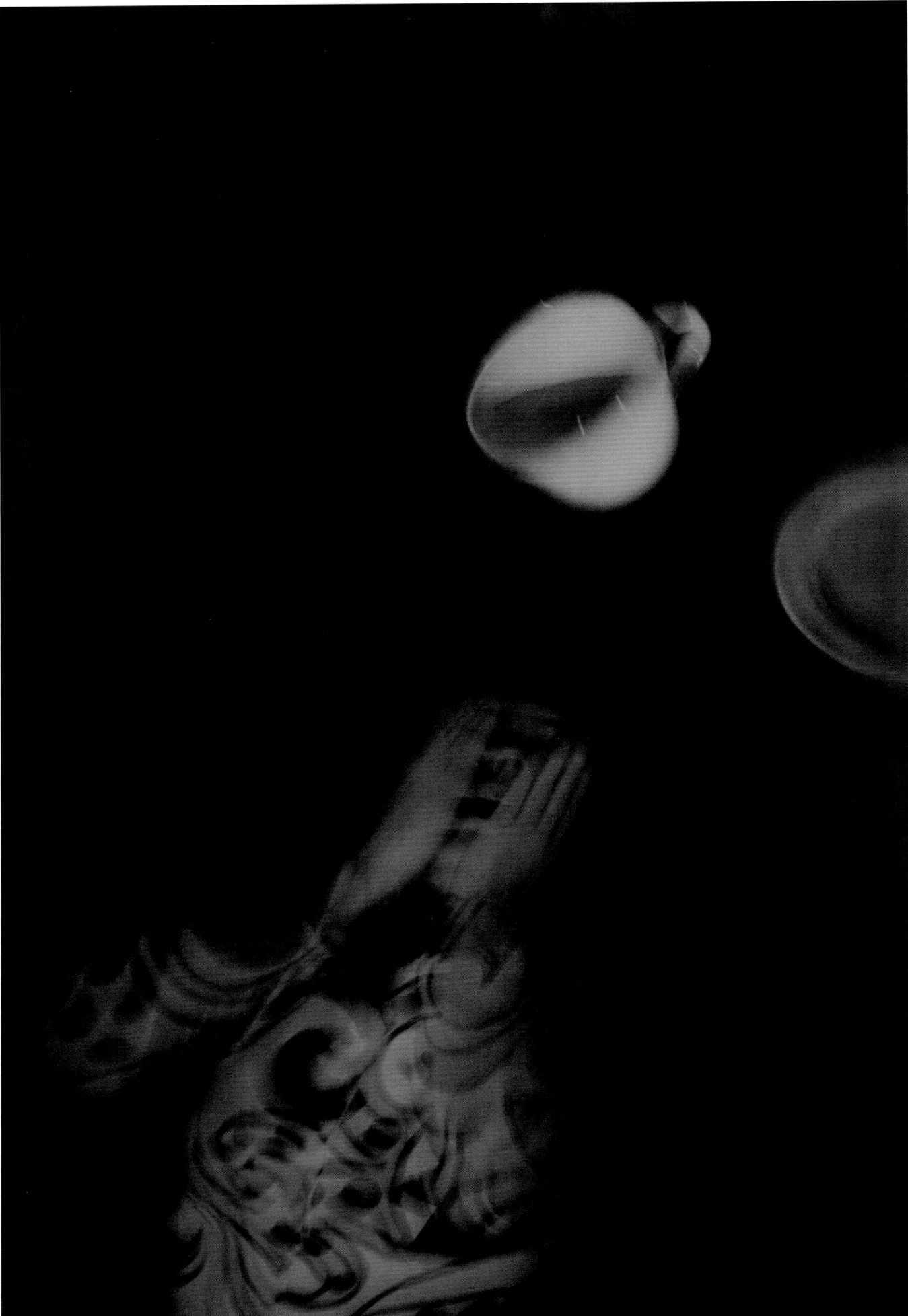

Anna & Bernhard Blume
Tellertraum from the series *Trautes Heim*
1988
Two black and white photographs
Each 79 × 49½ in. (200.7 × 125.7 cm)

ABOVE

Giuseppe Penone
Unghiata (Finger Work)
2003
Carrara marble panel
78¾ × 35⅜ × 1⅝ in. (199.9 × 89.9 × 4.1 cm)

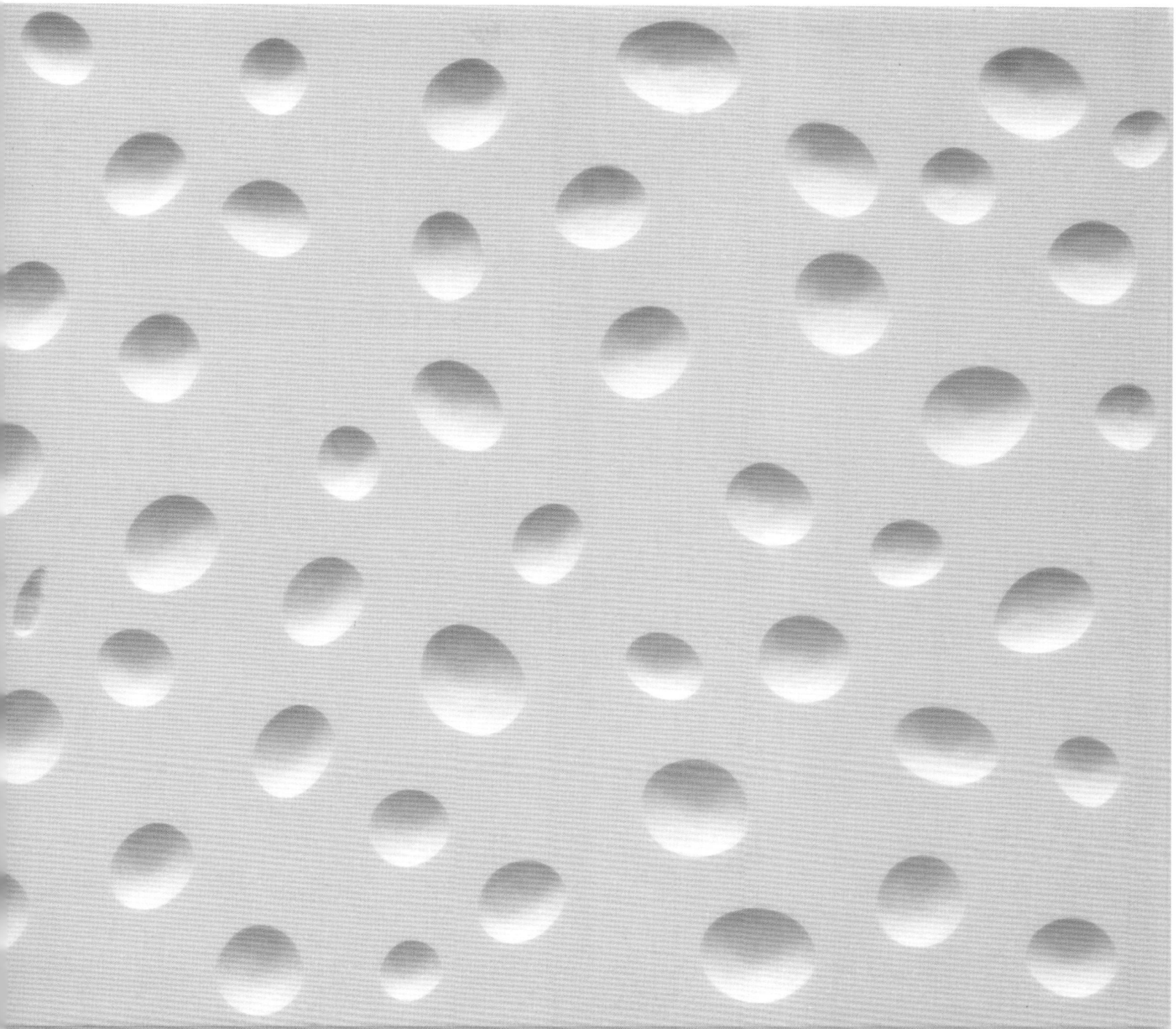

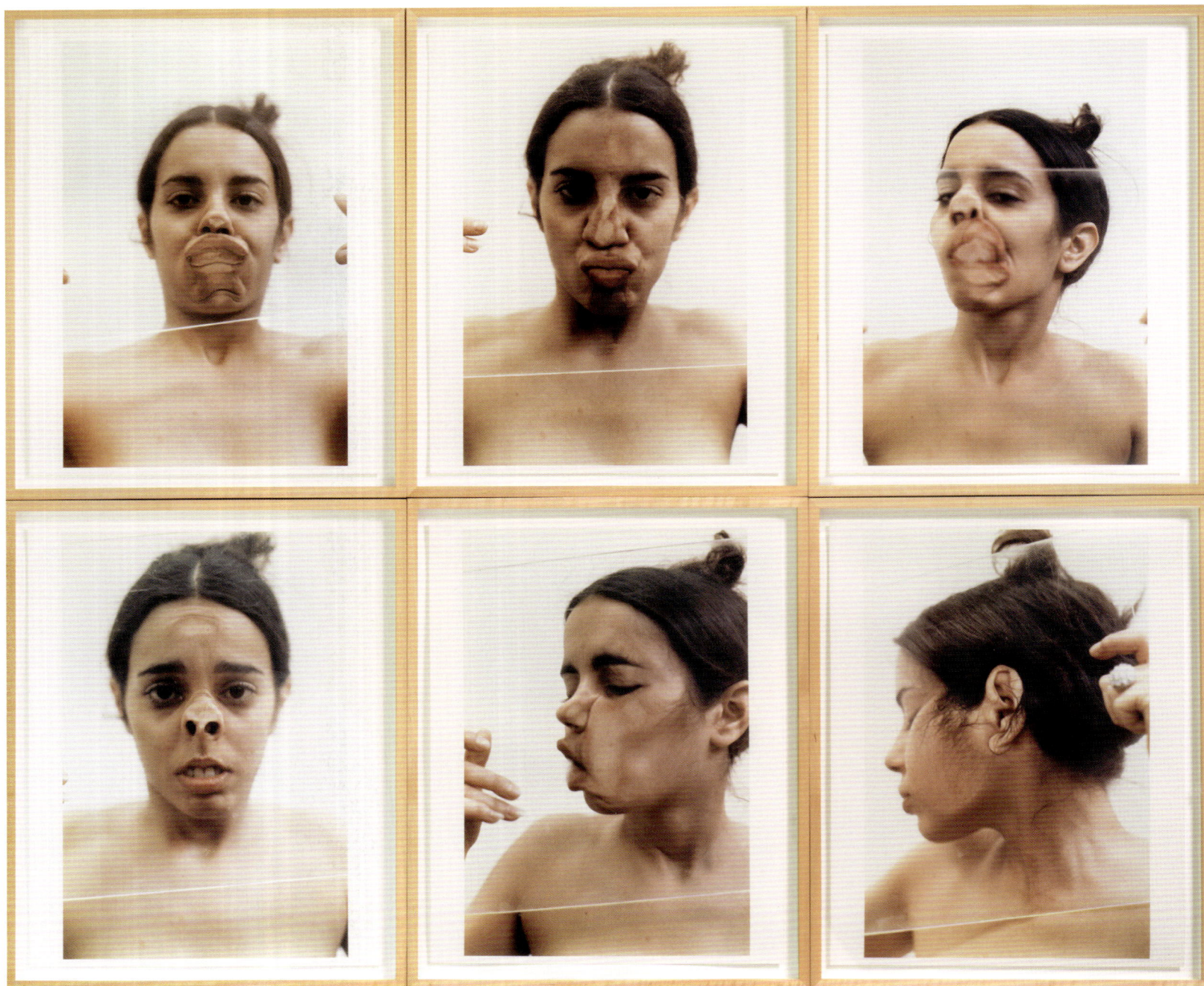

Ana Mendieta
Untitled (Glass on Body Imprints)
1972
Six color photographs
Each 19¼ × 12¾ in. (48.9 × 32.4 cm)

Scott Burton

A Unique Pair of Cubes
Laminated and lacquered plywood
Each 20 × 20 × 20 in. (50.8 × 50.8 × 50.8 cm)

Ken Lum
McGill & Son
2001
Plexiglass, powder coated aluminum,
plastic letters, enamel paint
48 × 120 in. (121.9 × 304.8 cm)

Philip-Lorca diCorcia

Head No. 4
2000
Fujicolor crystal archive print
48 × 60 in. (121.9 × 152.4 cm)

Platino
Extern 70.1
1988–97
C-print, acrylic, aluminum, plywood
92½ × 61½ in. × 1 in. (235 × 156.2 ×
2.5 cm)

Franz West
Untitled
1990
Painted by Marcus Geiger
Oil, gauze, cardboard
69 × 42 × 16 in. (175.3 × 106.7 × 40.6 cm)

ABOVE

Francis Alÿs
Camgun (Gun No. 16)
2005–6
In collaboration with Angel Toxqui
Wood, metal, plastic, film reels, film
16⅝ × 19¼ × 40 in. (42.2 × 48.9 × 101.6 cm)

FACING PAGE

Doris Salcedo
Untitled
1992
Wood, concrete, metal
47½ × 17¼ in. (120.7 × 43.8 cm)

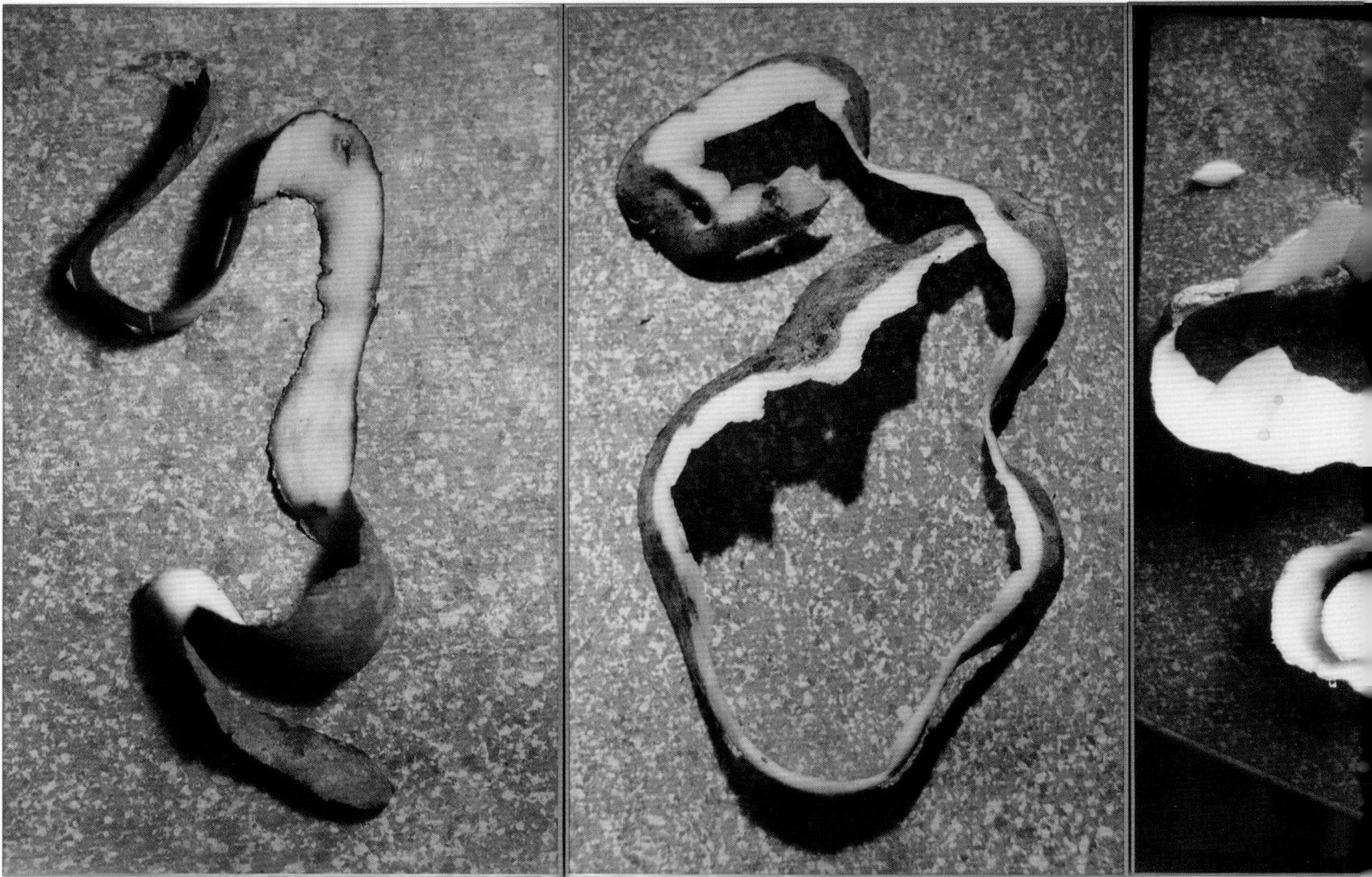

Anna & Bernhard Blume

Kartoffelschrift (Potato Peel)

1985–92

Five black and white photographs

Each 79 × 50 in. (200.7 × 127 cm)

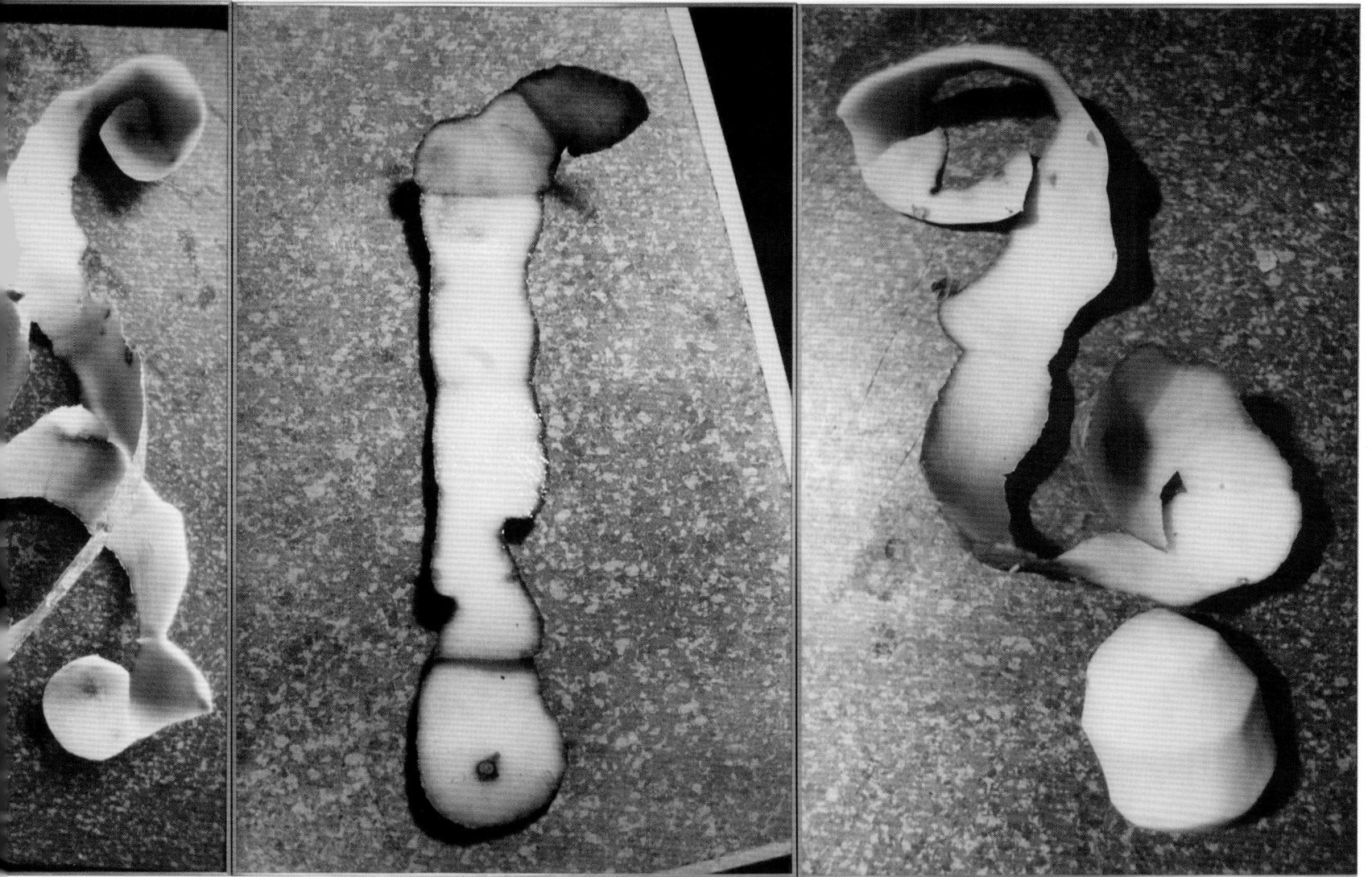

ABOVE

Platino
Extern 77.2
1980–2000
C-print, acrylic, aluminum, plywood
59 × 39⅜ × 1⅛ in. (149.9 × 100.1 × 3 cm)

FACING PAGE

Zheng Guogu
Calligraphy Waterfall
2006
Wax, newspaper, manuscripts
63 × 54½ × 54 in. (160 × 138.4 × 137.2 cm)

Liu Wei

Landscape - Celestial Mountain

2004

Five gelatin silver prints

Each 48⅛ × 120⅛ in. (123.2 × 306.1 cm)

Lynette Yiadom-Boakye
Since
2006
Oil on linen
78¾ × 70¾ in. (200 × 180 cm)

Lynette Yiadom-Boakye
Trawler
2011
Oil on canvas
98 × 78 in. (248.9 × 198.1 cm)

Thomas Ruff
55 Degrees
1990
C-print
101½ × 73 in. (257.8 × 185.4 cm)

Nate Lowman
Fallon
2005
Digital C-print mounted on Sintra
71¹⁄₁₆ × 51¹⁄₁₆ in. (180.5 × 129.7 cm)

ENTRANCE GALLERY

Stephan Balkenhol

Man and Woman

1999

Painted wood, two parts

Each 63¼ × 11⅝ in. (160.7 × 29.5 cm)

Sabrina Mezzaqui

The Arabian Nights
2004
Pages of *The Arabian Nights* rolled up, glue, thread
246 ft. (75 m)

Damián Ortega
Margin of Accident / Running Gag II
2005
Four wooden chairs
35½ × 16⅛ × 51⅝ in. (90.2 × 40.9 × 131.1 cm)

Andreas Gursky
Autobahn, Mettmann
1993
C-print
71¼ × 86 in. (180.7 × 218.4 cm)

Huang Yong Ping

Wells

2007

Glazed ceramic, taxidermy, in three parts

61 × 26½ (154.9 × 67.3), 51 × 23½ (129.5 × 59.7),

61 × 26 in. (154.9 × 66 cm)

FACING PAGE

Erik Schmidt

Einzelkämpfer mit Kugelfang
2006
Oil on canvas
74¾ × 51¼ in. (189.9 × 129.9 cm)

ABOVE

Thomas Struth

Paradise 7, Daintree, Australia
1998
C-print
68 × 88½ in. (172.7 × 224.8 cm)
© Thomas Struth

Mark Dion
The Great Chain of Being
1998
Red and blue pencil on paper
13 × 15 in. (33 × 38.1 cm)

Mark Dion

The Great Chain of Being

1998

Wooden cabinet, artifacts, botanical and zoological specimens, objets d'art, rocks, minerals, fungi, various bones

114 × 144 × 16 in. (289.6 × 365.8 × 40.6 cm)

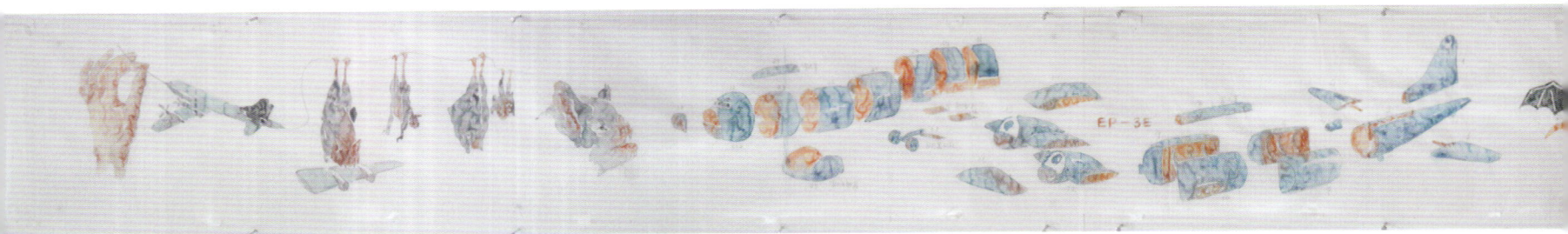

Huang Yong Ping
Long Drawing of the Bat Project
2003
Watercolor and ink on paper
3 × 13 × 220½ in. (7.6 × 33 × 560.1 cm)

Liz Deschenes
*Beppu No. 7, No. 3, No. 19, No. 10, No. 1,
No. 9,* and *No. 5*
1997
Seven Fujiflex prints
Each 19½ × 15½ in. (49.5 × 39.4 cm) or
the reverse

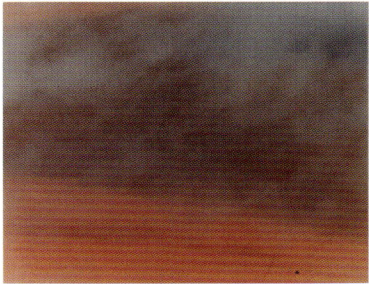

Huang Yong Ping

Chapeau à huit pattes (Eight-Legged Hat)
2000
Hat, watercolor, ink, wood, paint, wire
24 × 34 × 34 in. (61 × 86.4 × 86.4 cm)

Huang Yong Ping

Shed Snake Skin

2009

Tempera on silk

40⅜ × 146⅞ in. (102.6 × 372.4 cm)

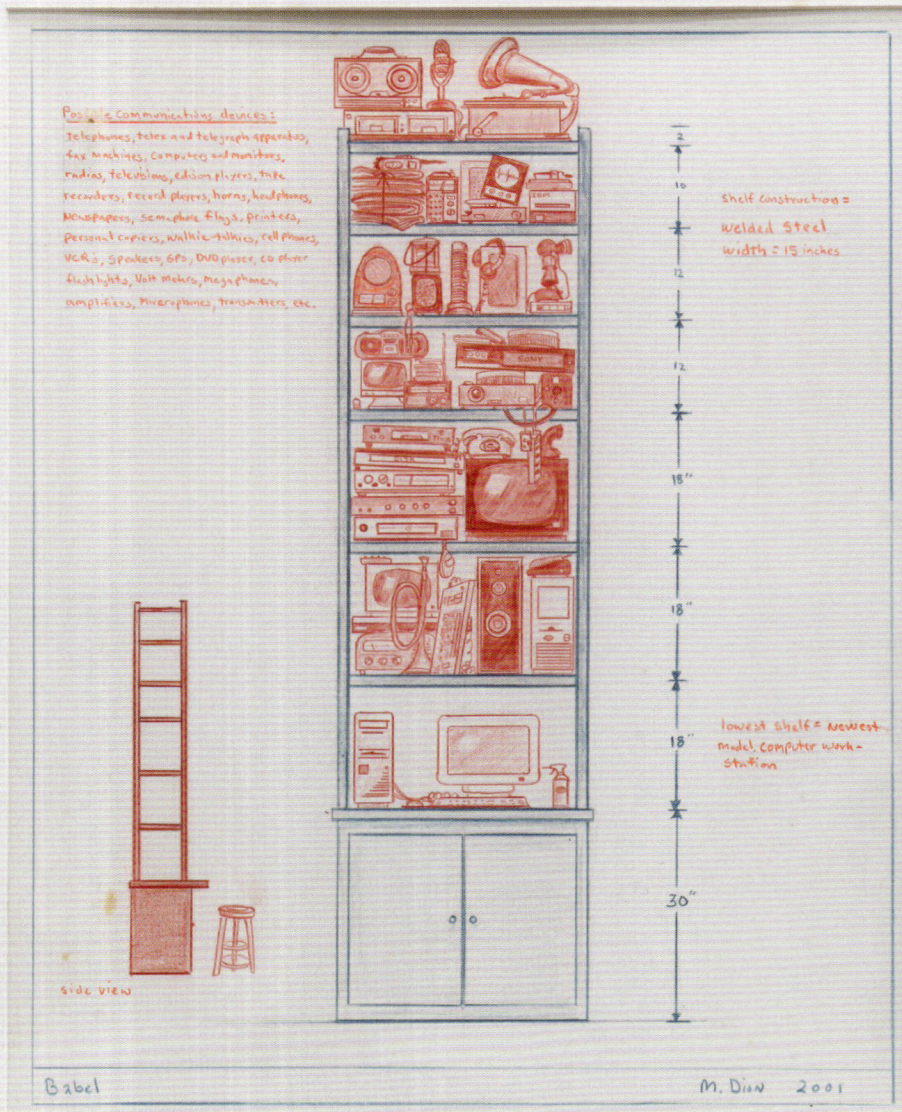

Mark Dion

Babel

2001

Red and blue pencil on paper

13½ × 10½ in. (34.3 × 26.7 cm)

Mark Dion

Babel

2002

Mixed media

144 × 36 × 30 in. (30.5 × 91.4 × 76.2 cm)

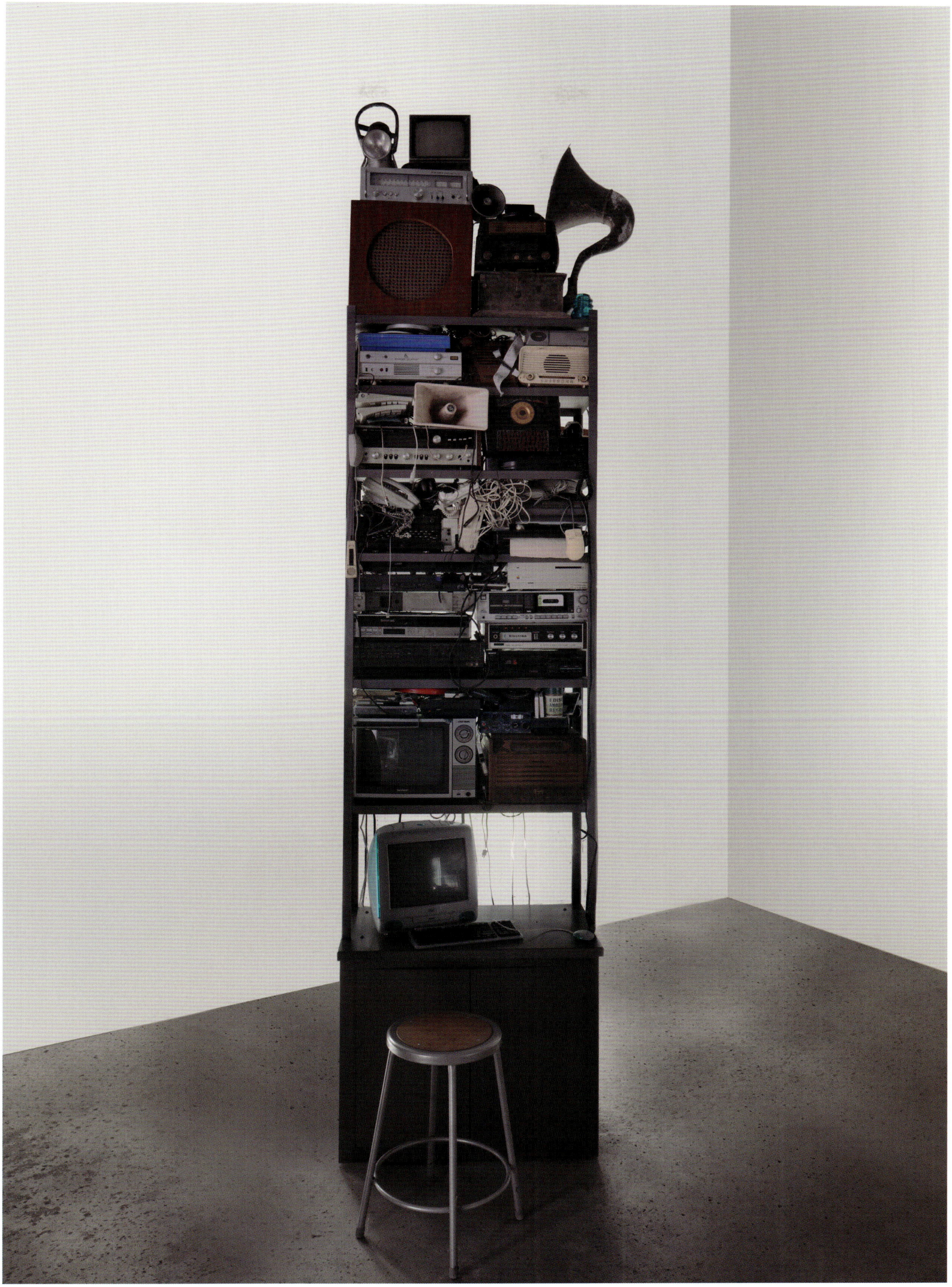

Paloma Varga Weisz

The Cabinet
2008
Wood barrel, coat hanger, wire, limewood, coat
74¾ × 55⅛ × 72 in. (189.9 × 140 × 182.9 cm)

STAGING
ROOM

A MoMA aff

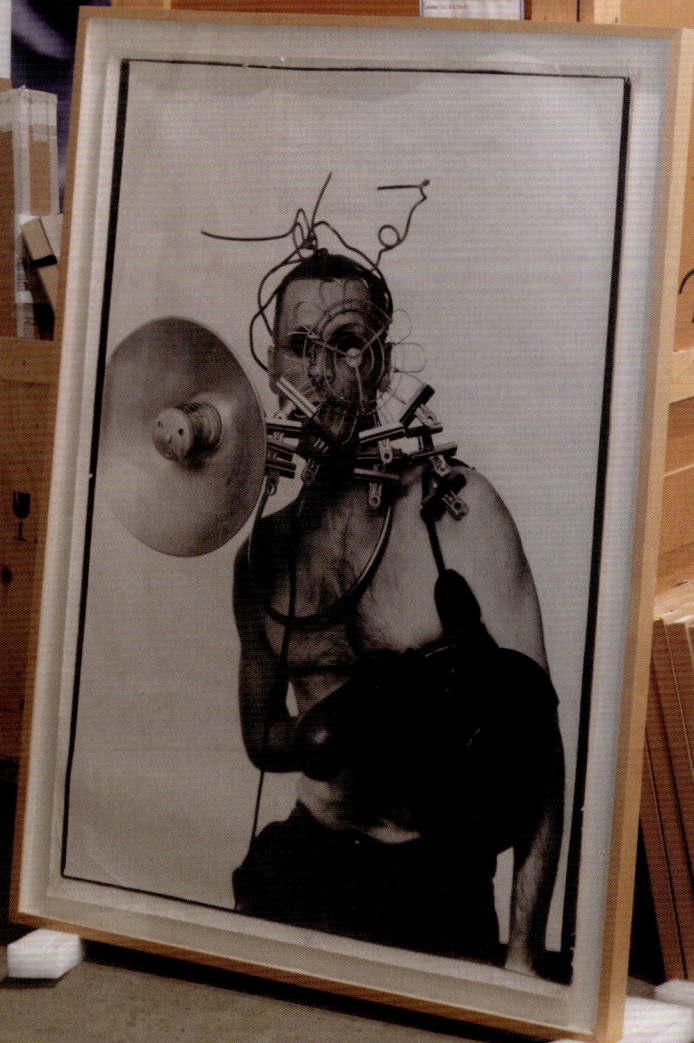

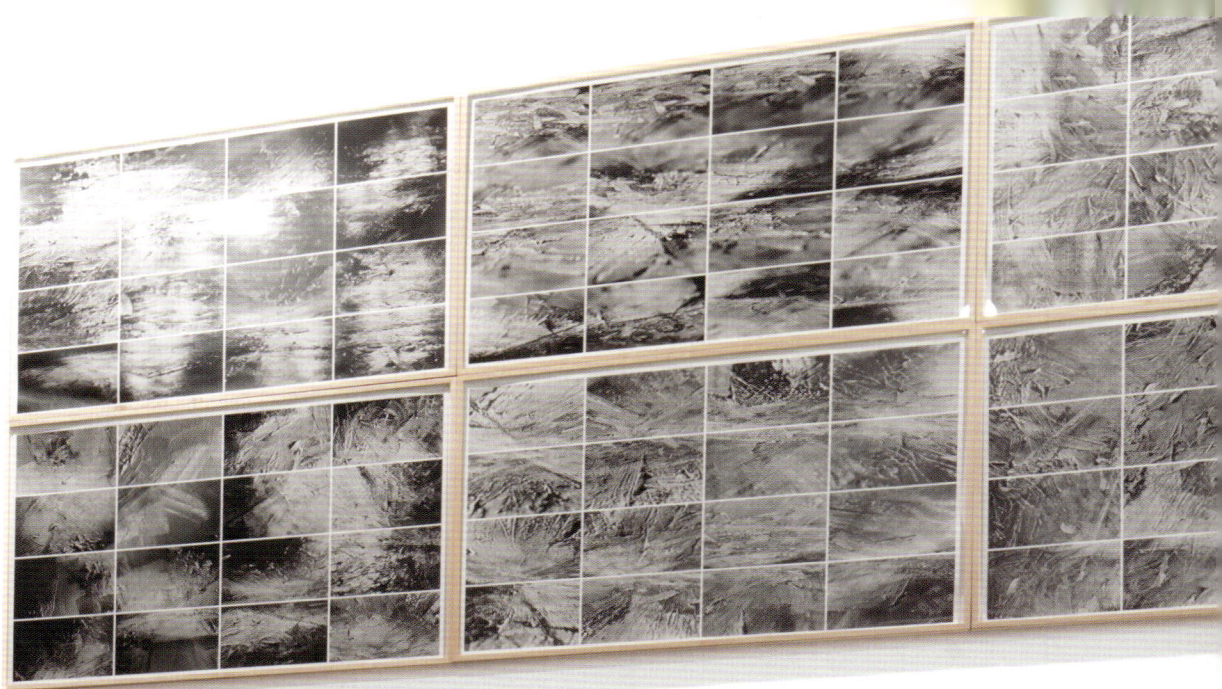

GLOBAL V

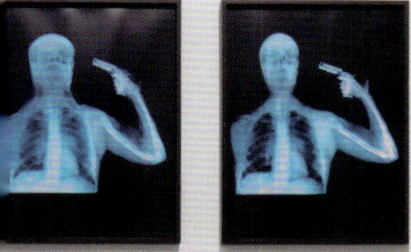

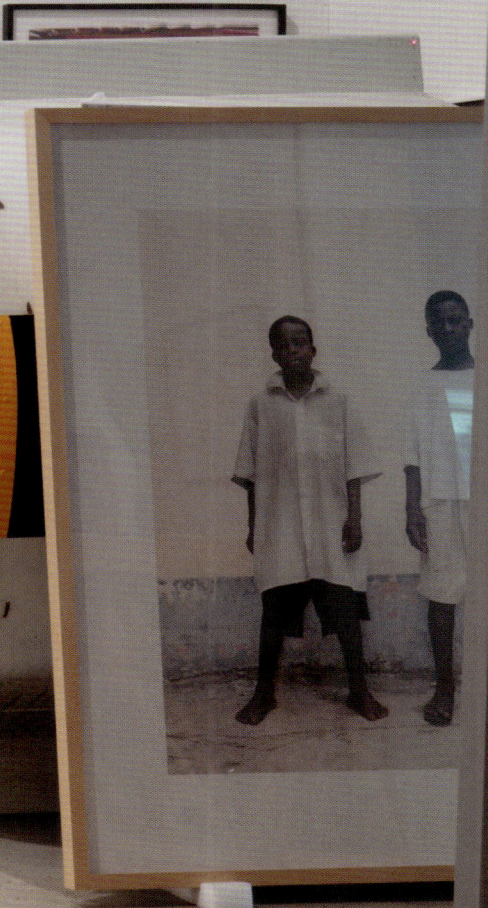

Anish Kapoor
Moonstone
1989
Slate, pigment
39 × 51 × 13 in. (99.1 × 129.5 × 33 cm)

FACING PAGE

Václav Stratil
From the cycle *Monastic Patient*
1991
Black and white photograph
38¼ × 25¾ in. (97 × 65.5 cm)

LOT-EK
TV-Tank, Section III
1998
Segment of a petroleum trailer tank, televisions, rubber tubing, foam, C-print, lumigraphic mounting system
74 × 92 × 54 in. (188 × 233.7 × 137.6 cm)

Lynn Davis
*Iceberg No. 30, Disko Bay, Green-
land, 2000*
2000
Selenium-toned gelatin silver print
40 × 40 in. (101.6 × 101.6 cm)

Philip-Lorca diCorcia
Eric Hutsell, 27 Years Old, Southern
California, $20
1994
Cibachrome print
20 × 24 in. (50.8 × 63.5 cm)

FACING PAGE

ABOVE

Hans Haacke

Mobil: On the Right Track
1980
Color screenprint on paper
60 × 43 in. (152.4 × 109.2 cm)

Mark Dion

Waterfowl, "Duck, Duck, Goose"
2002
Duck decoys, dry plants, wood, crate, tar
72 × 34 × 34 in. (182.9 × 86.4 × 86.4 cm)

Bertozzi & Casoni

Cover

2003

Glazed ceramic

23¼ × 16½ × 19 in. (59.1 × 41.9 × 48.3 cm)

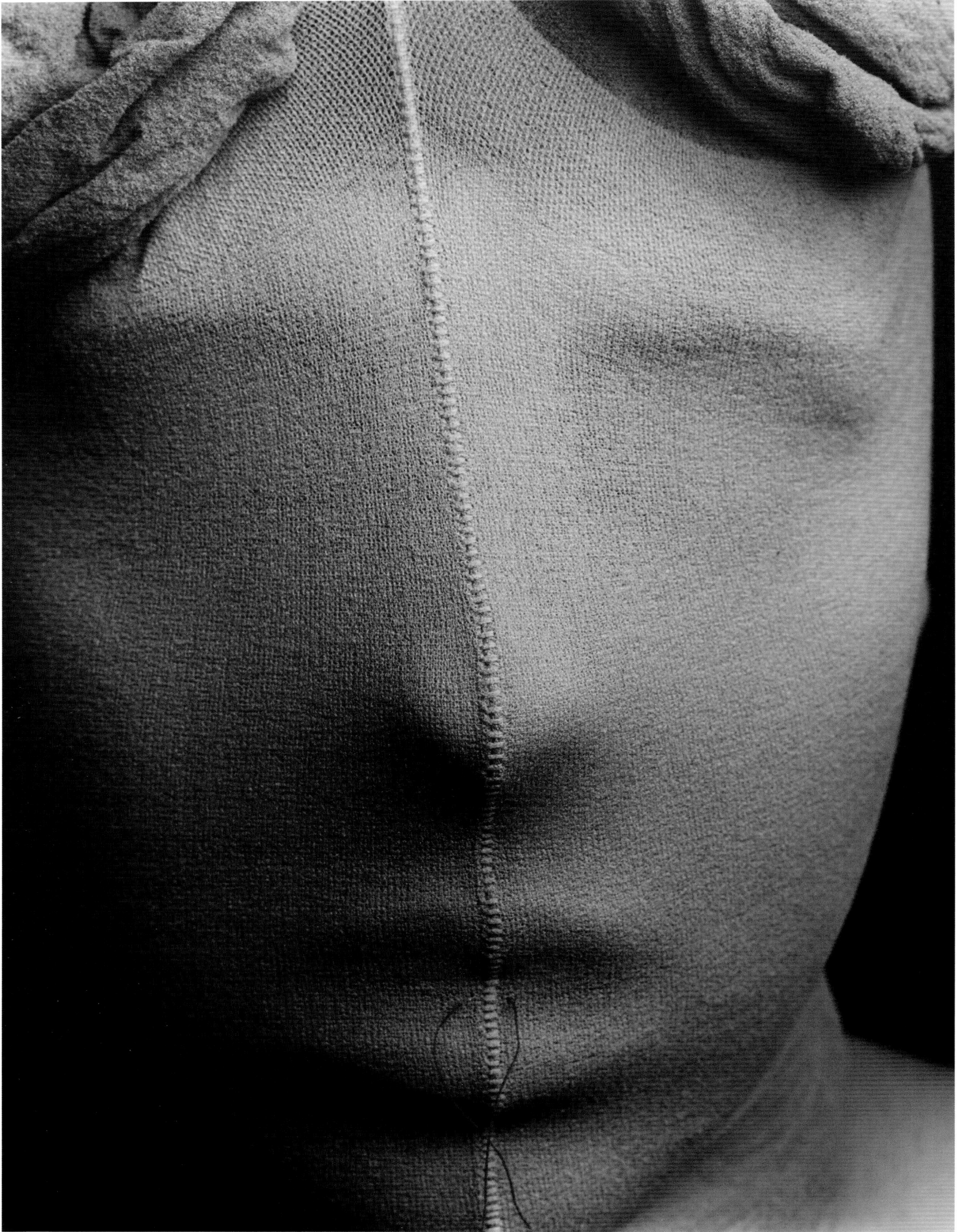

A MoMA affiliate

Justine Reyes
Untitled No. 13
2004
C-print
40 × 30 in. (101.6 × 76.2 cm)

Nate Lowman
A MoMA Affiliate
2006
Alkyd on canvas
60 × 72 in. (152.4 × 182.9 cm)

ABOVE

Wolfgang Tillmans
after party (a)
2002
C-print
20 × 24 in. (50.8 × 61 cm)

FACING PAGE

Ján Mančuška
Chair
2001
Wood, plastic sheeting, corner
braces, nails
39½ × 21 × ½ in. (100.3 × 53.3 × 1.3 cm)

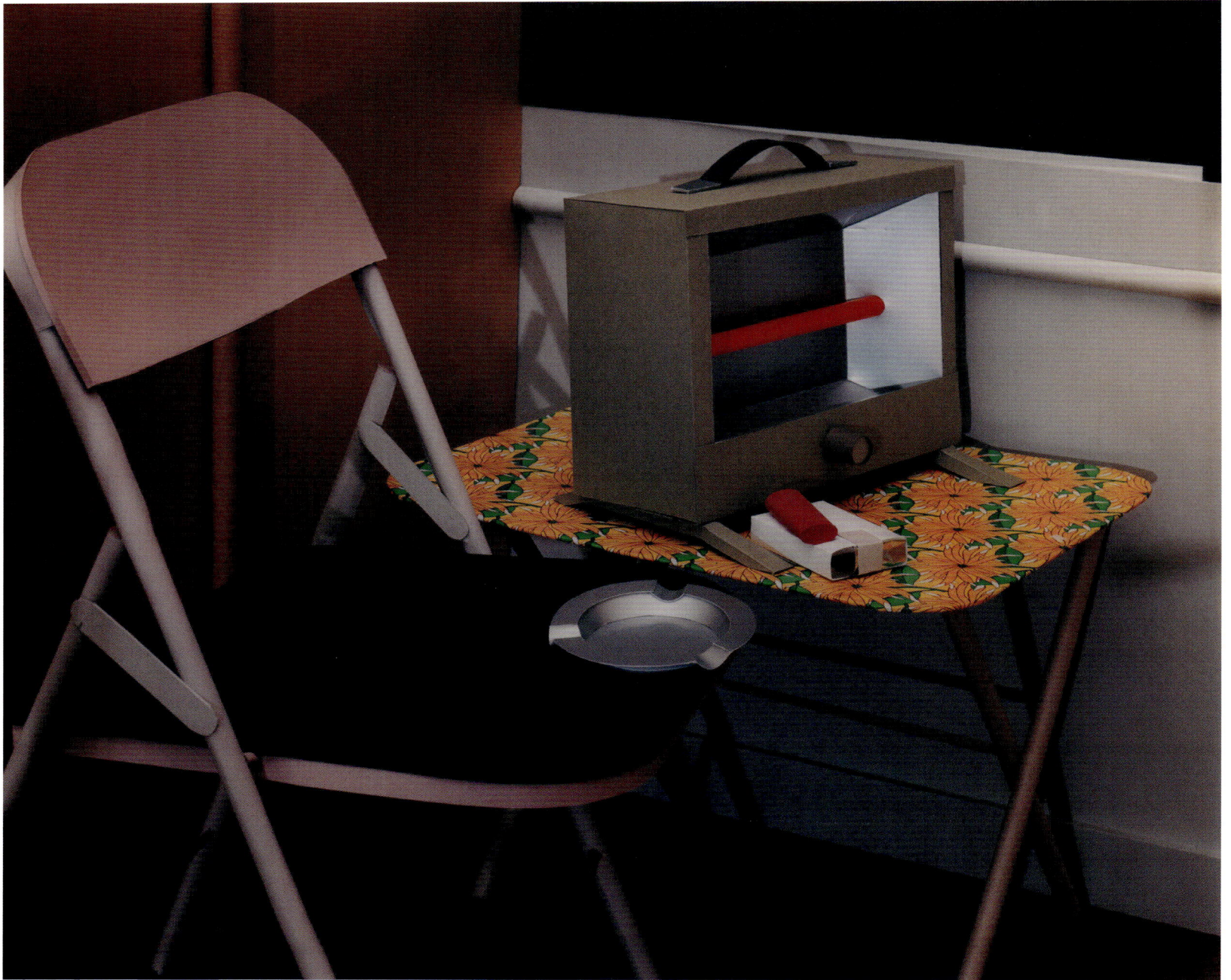

Thomas Demand
Detail V (Salon)
2000
C-print on Diasec
76½ × 92 in. (194.3 × 233.7 cm)

Thomas Demand
Pile (Stapel), from the portfolio
Double Exposure
2001–2
Two Lambda prints
Each approx. 23½ × 19¾ in. (59.7 × 50 cm)

Gregor Zivic

Untitled

1999

C-print on aluminum

49⅛ × 52 in. (125.2 × 132.1 cm)

Frank Breuer
Untitled
2006
C-print
30 × 36 in. (76.2 × 91.4 cm)

Peter Garfield
Mobile Home (Ranch)
1994
Chromogenic print
16 × 20 in. (40.6 × 50.8 cm)

Beate Gütschow
LS No. 7
1993
C-print
64⅜ × 45⅝ in. (163.5 × 115.9 cm)

Michael Wesely
New York Vertical, Square Meals
1995
C-print on aluminum
99 × 48¼ in. (251.5 × 123.2 cm)

Frank Thiel
Stadt 9/31/D (Berlin)
2001
C-print
118 × 63 in. (299.7 × 160 cm)

Candida Höfer

Naturkundemuseum Tilburg III 1994

1994

C-print

14 × 14¼ in. (35.6 × 36.2 cm)

Candida Höfer
Bibliothek Reiner Speck III 2000
2000
C-print
23⅝ × 23⅝ in. (59.9 × 59.9 cm)

Roman Signer

Progression of Brown Paper

1981

Four black and white photographs on Baryta paper

Each 14⅛ × 9½ in. (35.8 × 24.1 cm)

LEFT

Peter Garfield
Harsh Reality II
1998
Black and white photograph
50 × 68 in. (127 × 172.7 cm)

PAGES 128–9

Roman Signer
Rocket Launch
1978
Two black and white photographs on
Baryta paper
Each 23¼ × 19¾ in. (59.2 × 50 cm)

Roman Signer
Large Forest with Bullet
1983
C-print
30 × 40 in. (76.2 × 101.6 cm)

Nobuyoshi Araki
Erotos
1993
Gelatin silver print
24 × 20 in. (61 × 50.8 cm)

John Coplans
Self-Portrait (Heel, Dark Sole), 1989
1989
Gelatin silver print
30 × 37 in. (76.2 × 94 cm)

Nobuyoshi Araki
Kinbaku (Bondage) Wide-Scarred Nude
1991
Gelatin silver print
24 × 20 in. (61 × 50.8 cm)

Hans Breder
Body/Sculpture
1971
Black and white photograph
15 × 14⅞ in. (38.1 × 37.8 cm)

Hans Breder
Body/Sculpture
1969–73
Black and white photograph
15 × 14⅞ in. (38.1 × 37.8 cm)

Hans Breder
Body/Sculpture
1971
Black and white photograph
mounted on paperboard
15 × 14⅞ in. (38.1 × 37.8 cm)

Hans Breder
Body/Sculpture
1970
Black and white photograph
mounted on paperboard
15 × 14⅞ in. (38.1 × 37.8 cm)

Carsten Höller

Braunes Bayer-Auge

2004

Inkjet print on glossy paper

23⅝ × 23⅝ in. (60 × 60 cm)

Thomas Ruff

Nudes WR28

2000

Laserchrome print

51 × 39¼ in. (129.5 × 99.8 cm)

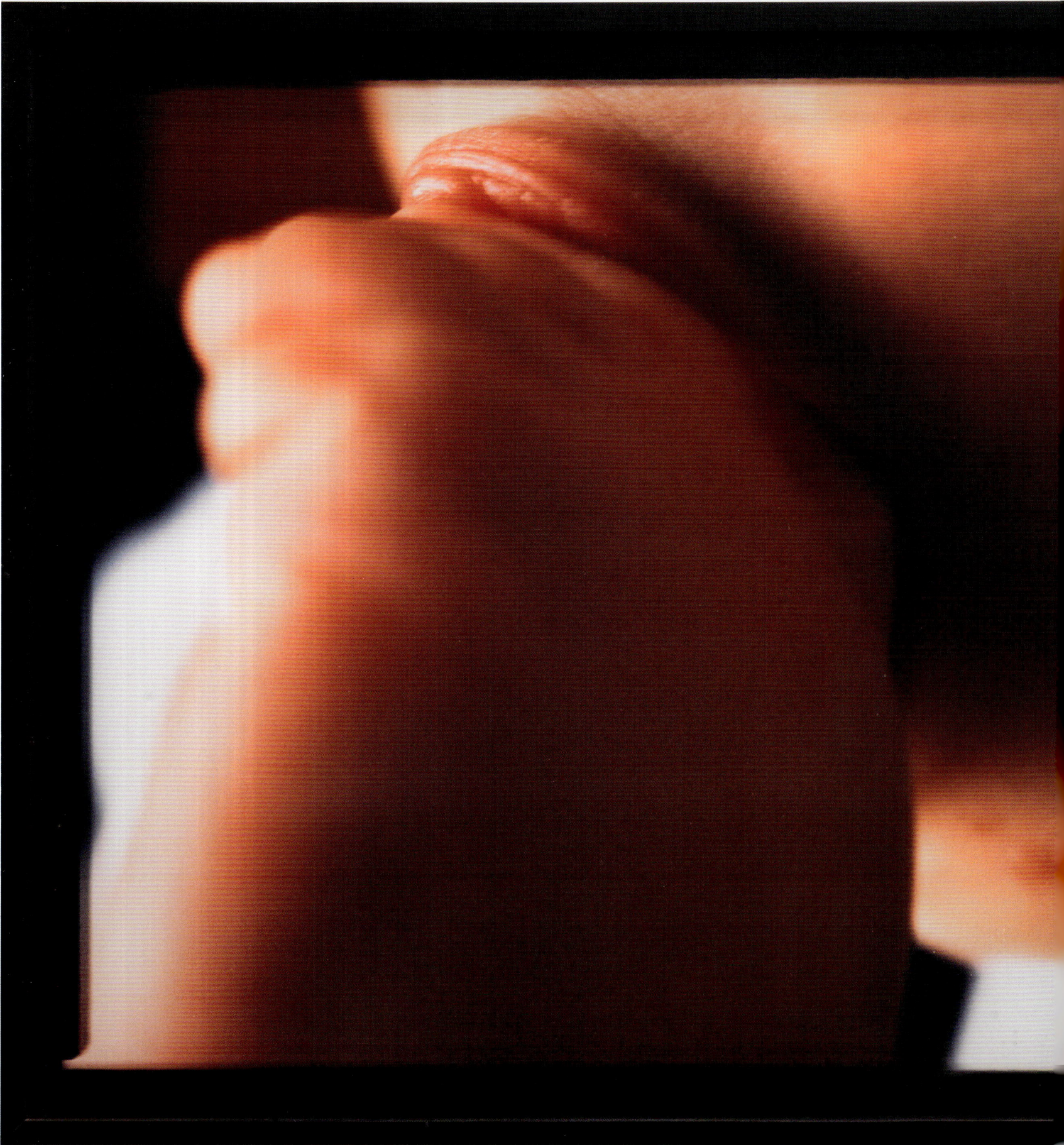

Douglas Gordon
Croque Mort
2000
C-print
38½ × 55½ in. (97.8 × 141 cm)

Wolfgang Laib
Pine Forest Near Artist's Studio
1981
Gelatin silver print
11 × 14 in. (27.9 × 35.6 cm)

Wolfgang Laib
Dandelion Meadow Near Artist's Studio
1981
Gelatin silver print
11 × 14 in. (27.9 × 35.6 cm)

Wolfgang Laib
Temple Water Basin near Shravanabelgola, India
2001
Gelatin silver print
12 × 16 in. (30.5 × 40.6cm)

PAGES 142–5

Gerhard Richter
128 Fotos von Einem Bild (Halifax 1978) II
1998
Portfolio of eight prints
Each 25¼ × 39½ in. (64.1 × 100.3 cm)

141

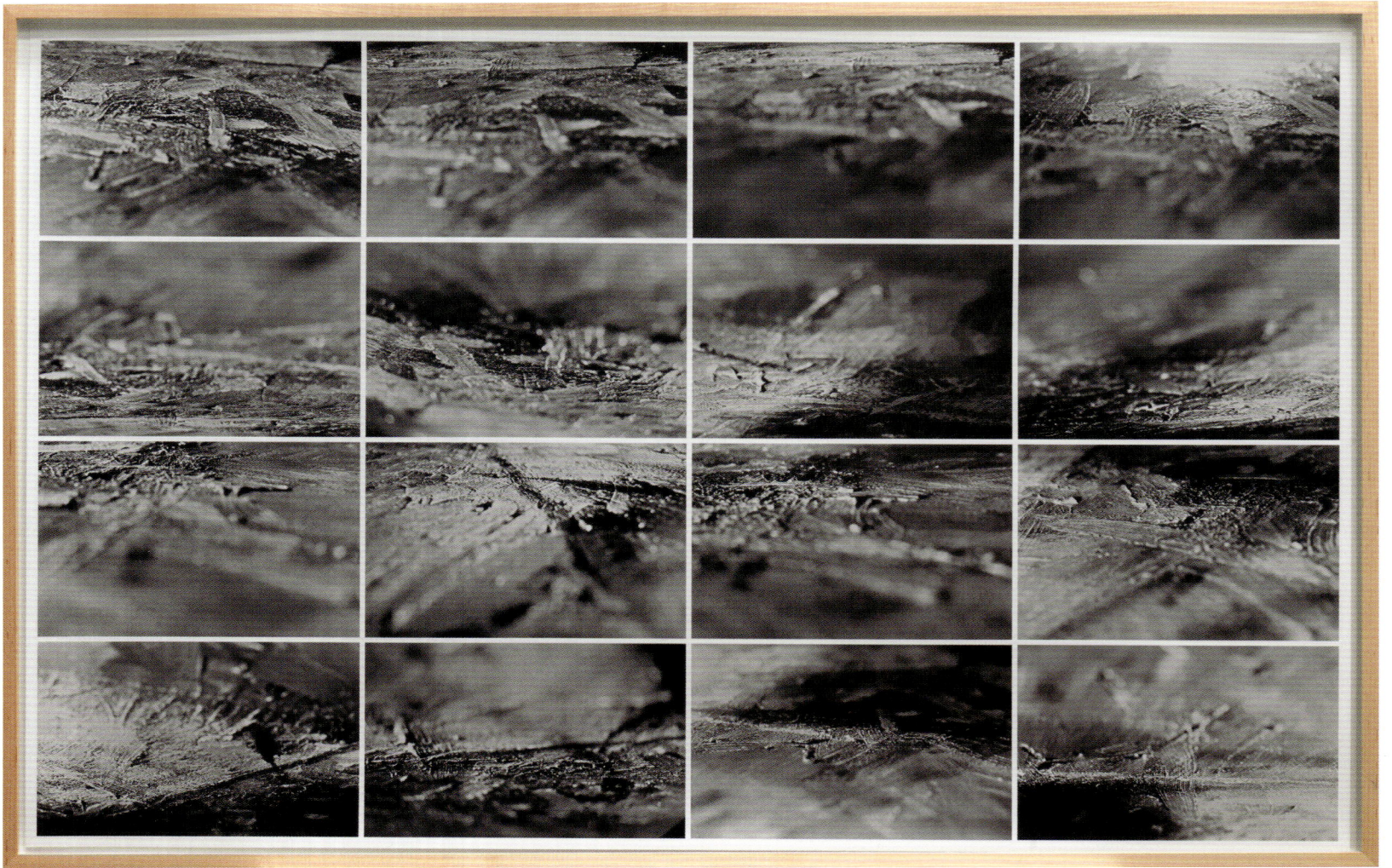

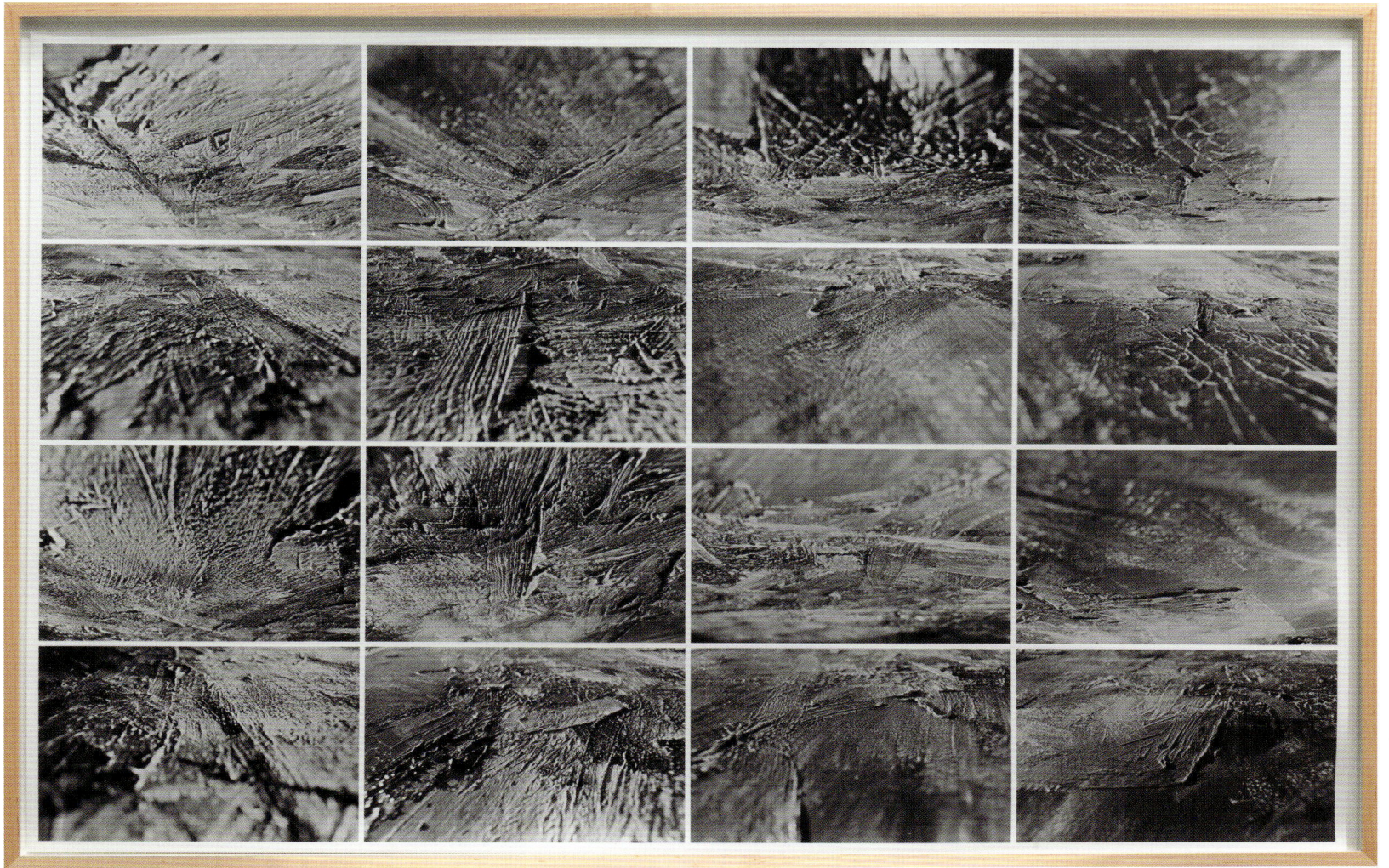

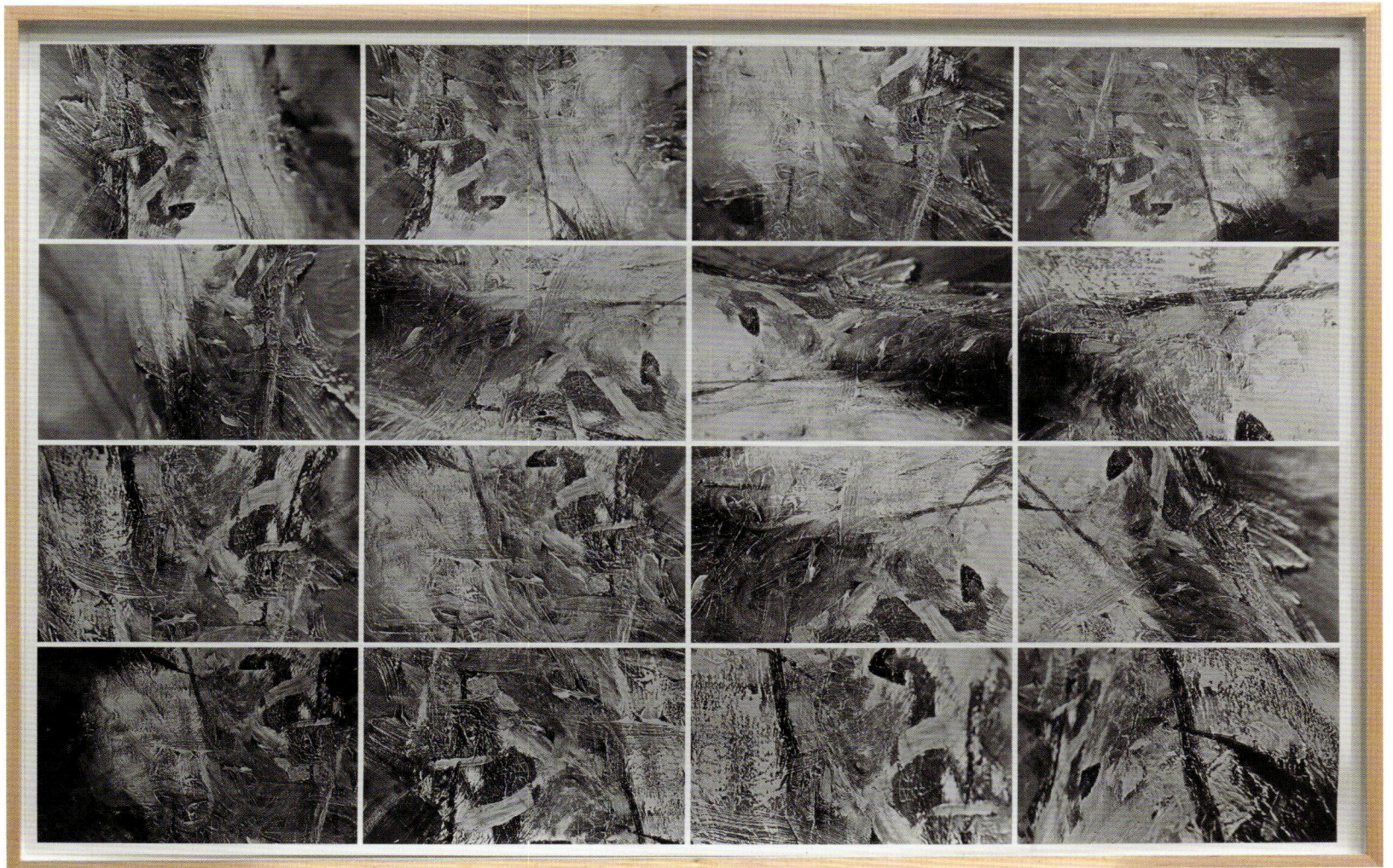

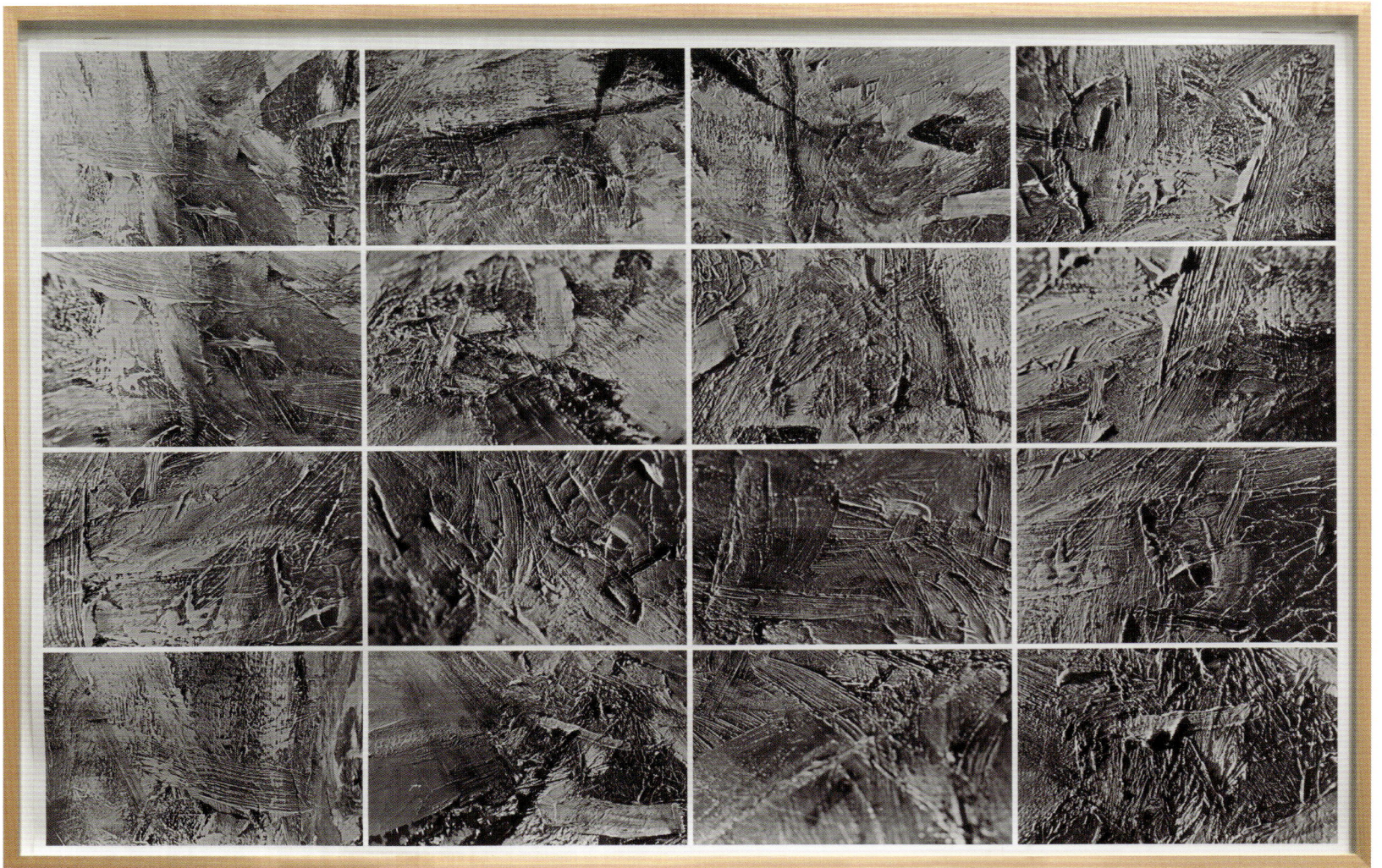
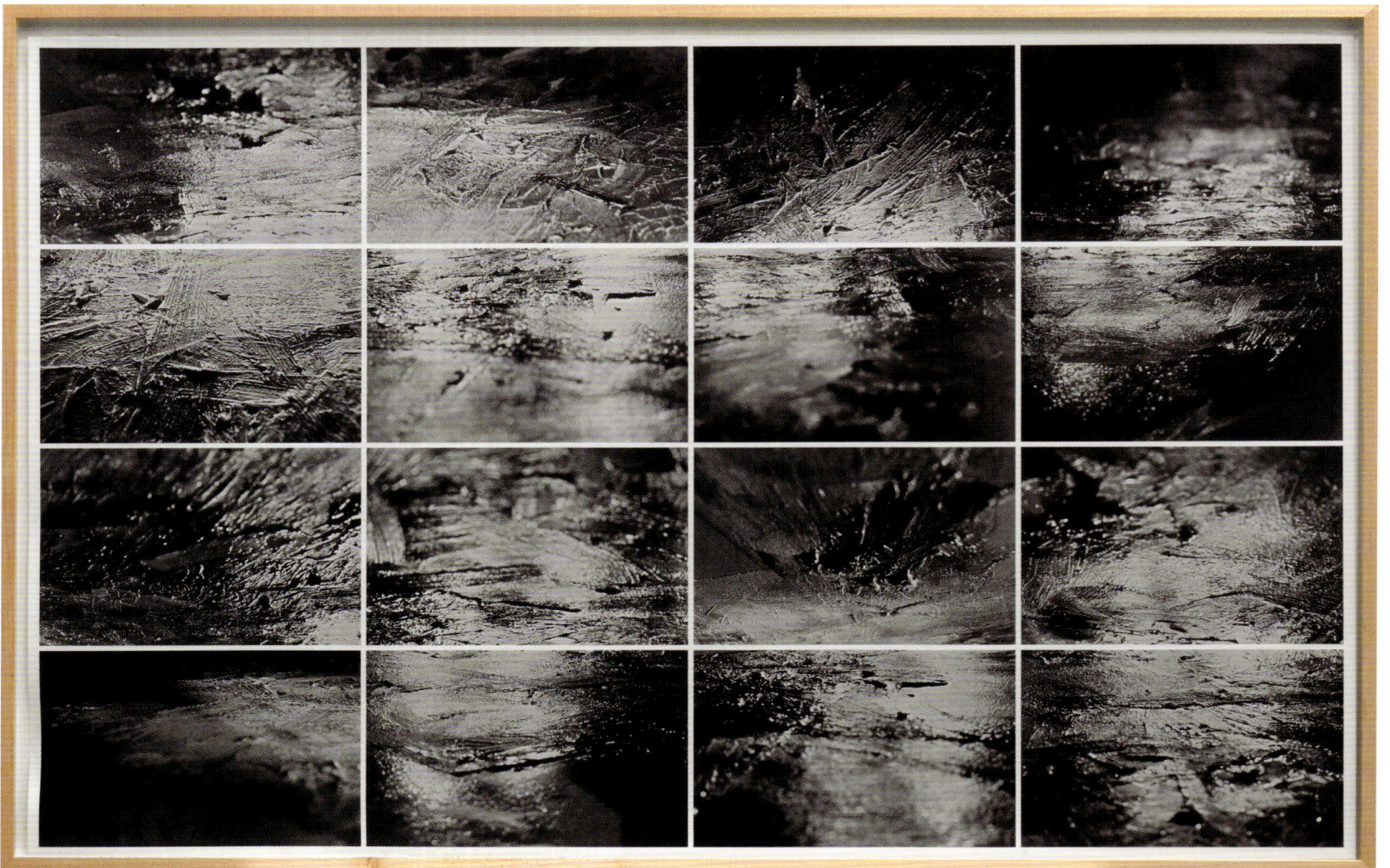

144

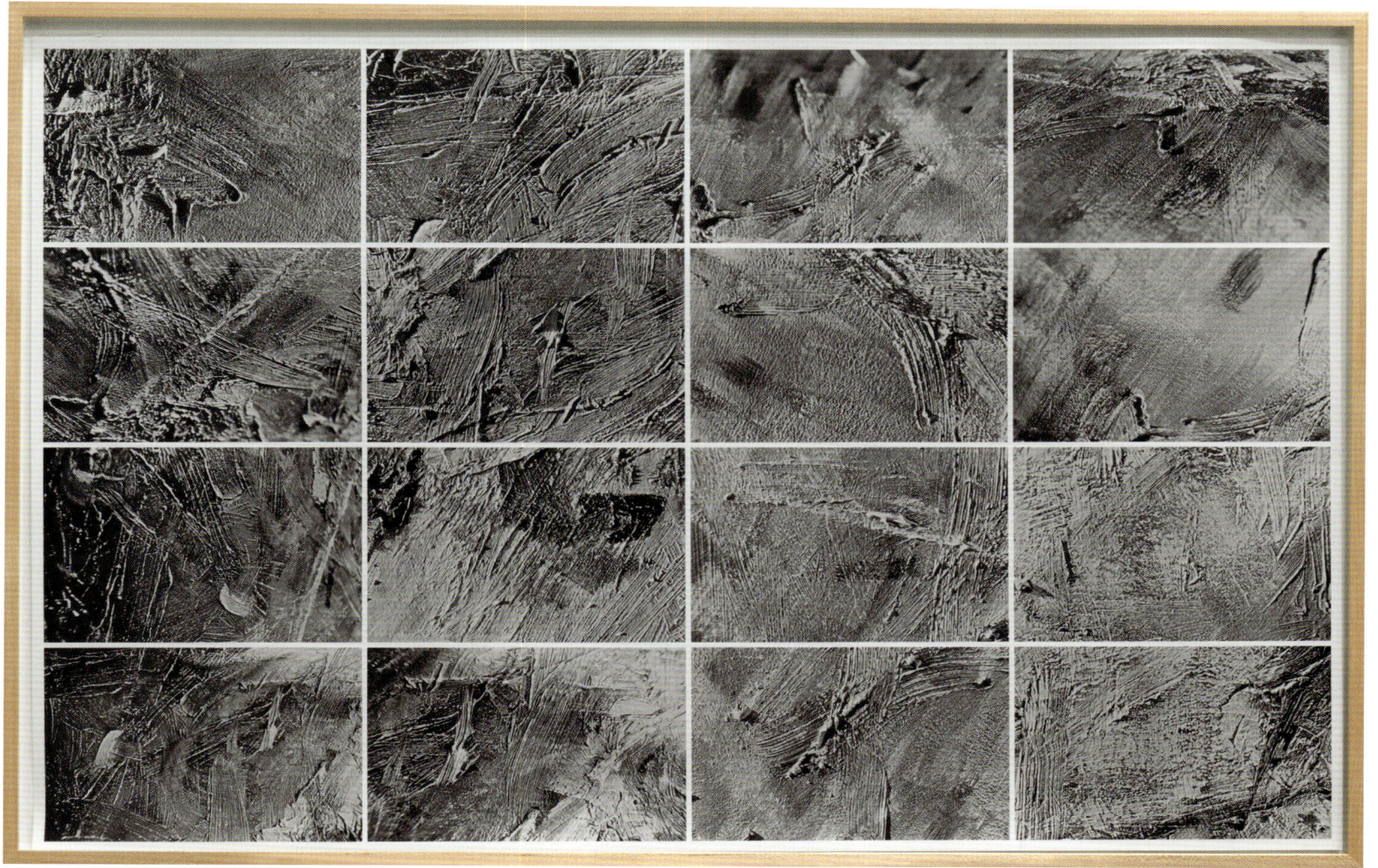
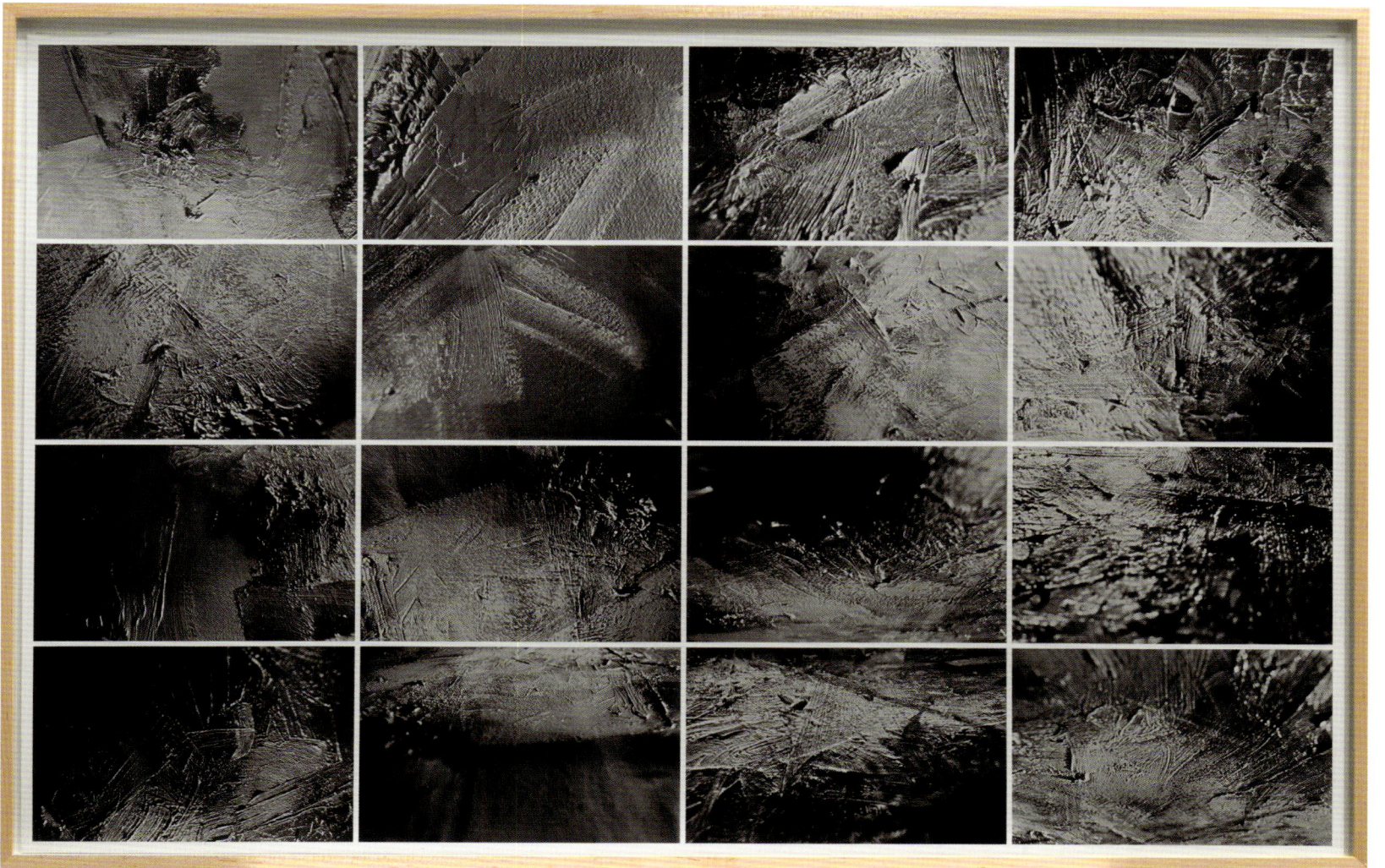

Massimo Vitali
Rosignano 3 Women
1995
C-print
59 × 71 in. (149.9 × 180.3 cm)

Tim Davis
Target, Connecticut
2001
C-print
30 × 40 in. (76.2 × 101.6 cm)

Anna & Bernhard Blume
Transzendentaler Konstruktivismus
1992–94
Black and white photograph sequence

David Robbins
The Naturalist
2003
Epson 10000 archival inkjet print
32 × 29⅛ in. (81.3 × 74.9 cm)

Lin Yilin

Future Relic – Guangzhou
2006
C-print
63¾ × 48 in. (161.9 × 121.9 cm)

Christoph Keller
Canal Street
2000
Lambda color photograph
11 × 118 in. (27.9 × 299.7 cm)

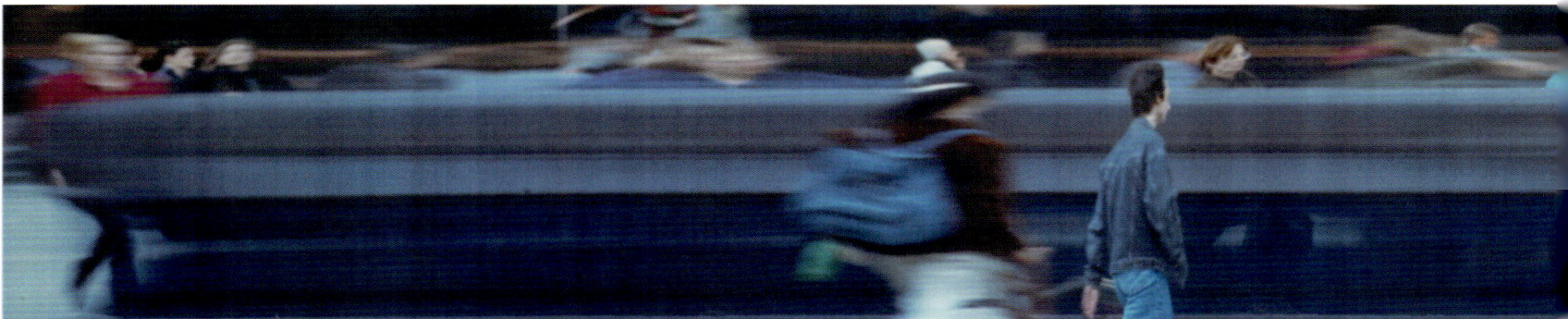

Christoph Keller
Menschen am Alex
2000
Lambda color photograph
5 × 48 in. (12.7 × 121.9 cm)

Rineke Dijkstra

Accra, Ghana, Africa, March 1, 1996
1996
Chromogenic print
61½ by 51¾ in. (156.2 by 131.4 cm)

Willie Bester

Crossroads

1994

Oil paint, rope, barbed wire,
ammunition, disassembled gun
parts mounted on board

31½ × 59 in. (80 × 149.9 cm)

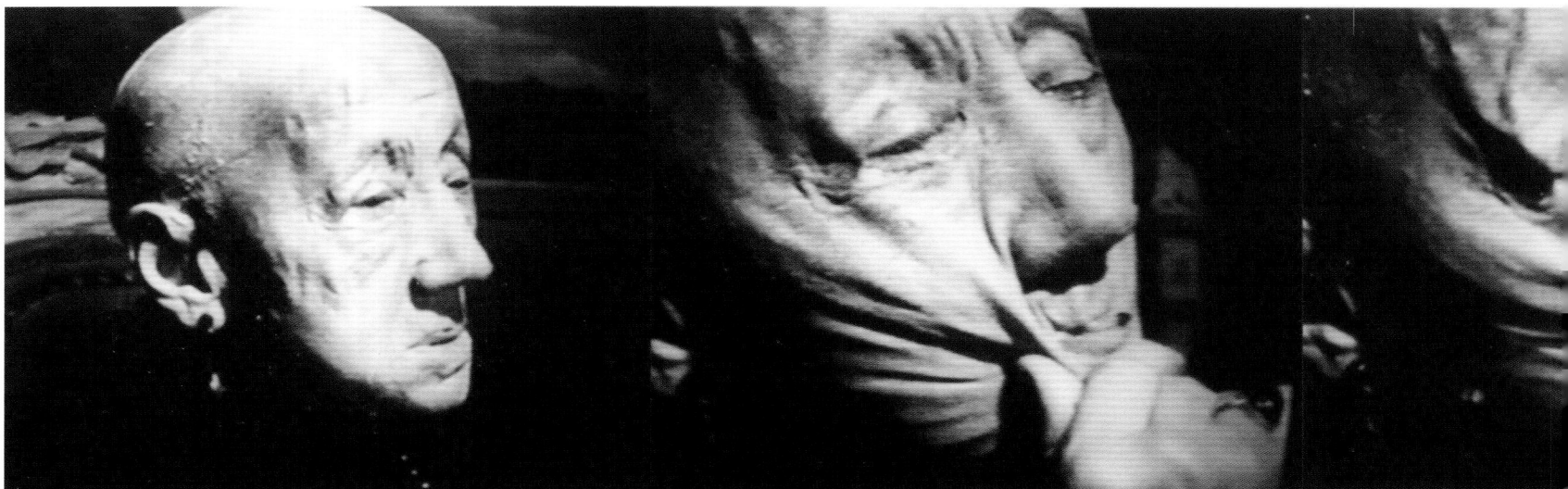

John Waters
Swedish Film
2000
Five silver gelatin prints
Each 8 × 10 in. (20.3 × 25.4 cm)

Olafur Eliasson
Untitled (Iceland Series)
2000 and 2001
Four C-prints
Each 25⅝ × 35½ in. (65 × 90.2 cm)

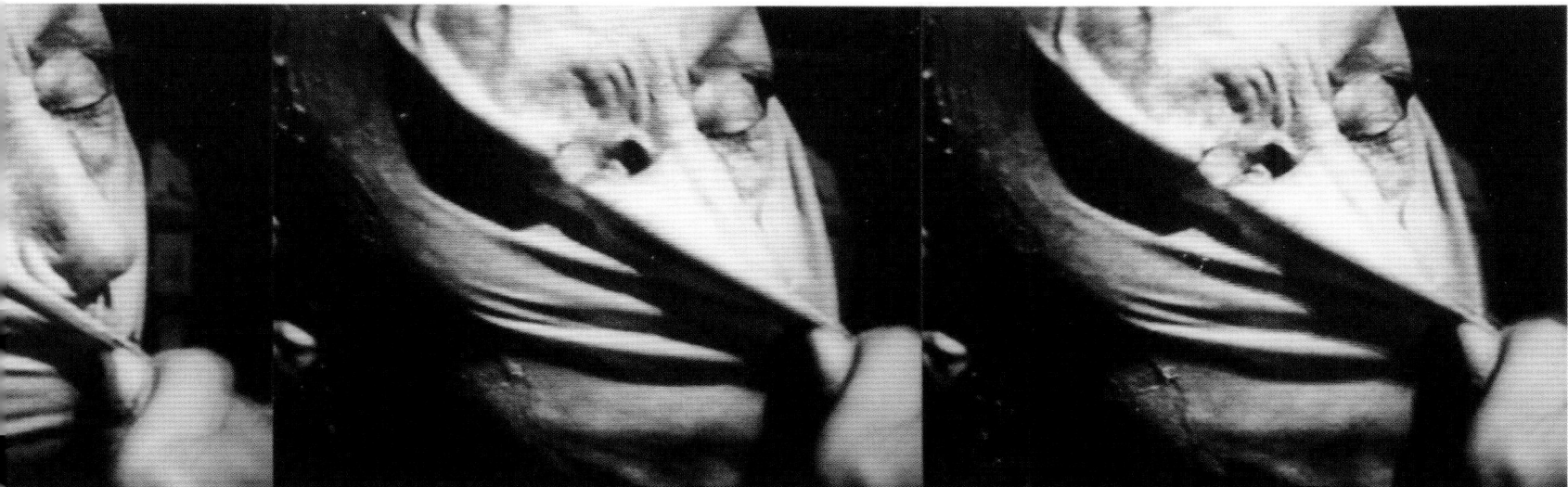

Nobuyoshi Araki

Sky, Bondage, Flower
2001/2002
Thirty Polaroids
Each 4½ × 4½ in. (11.43 × 11.43 cm)

Nobuyoshi Araki

Colourscapes

1991–2005

Eighteen C-prints

Each 15 × 23 in. (38.1 × 58.4 cm)

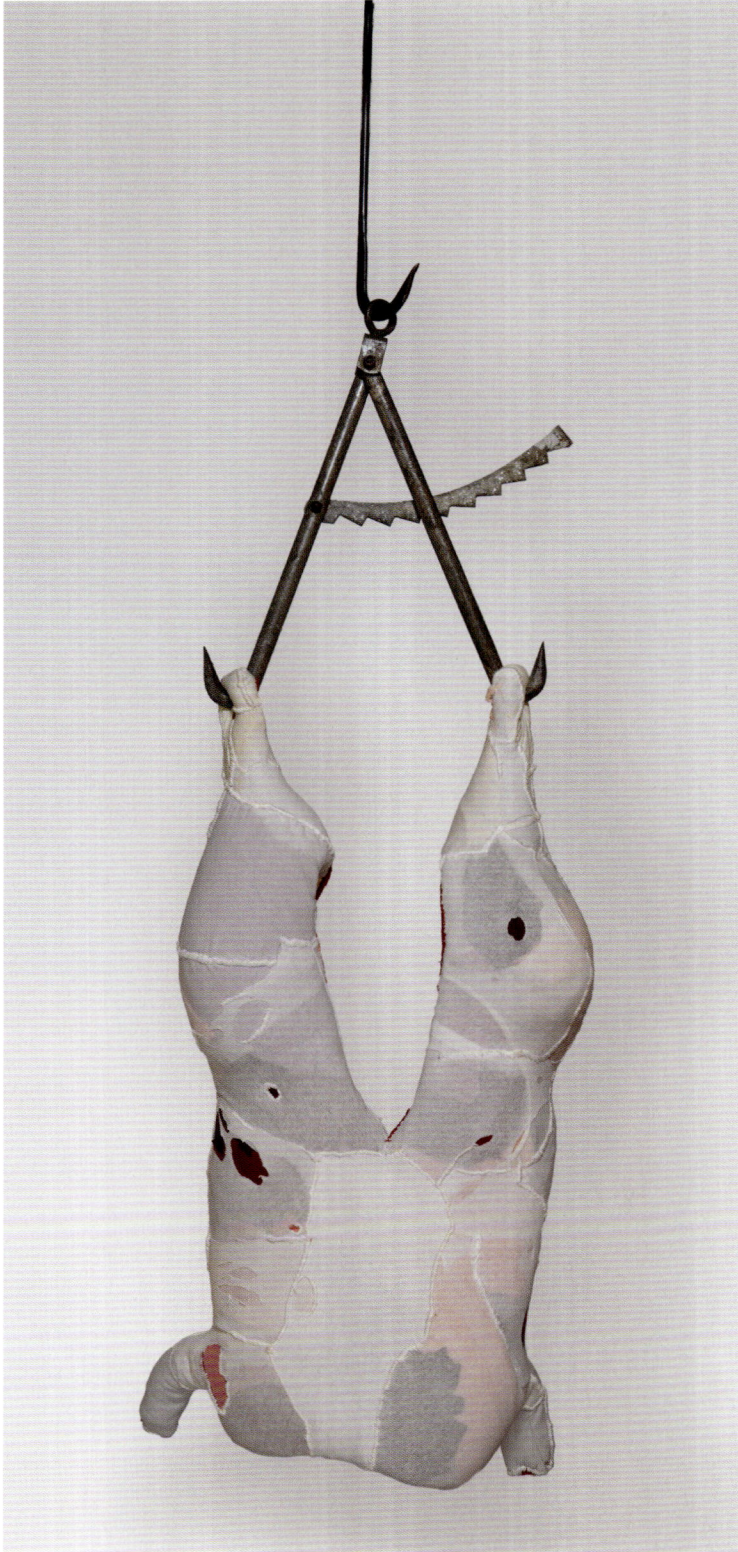

Tamara Kostianovsky

Second Skin

2007

Artist's clothing, embroidery, floss batting wire,
meat hook

60 × 29 × 12 in. (152.4 × 73.7 × 30.5 cm)

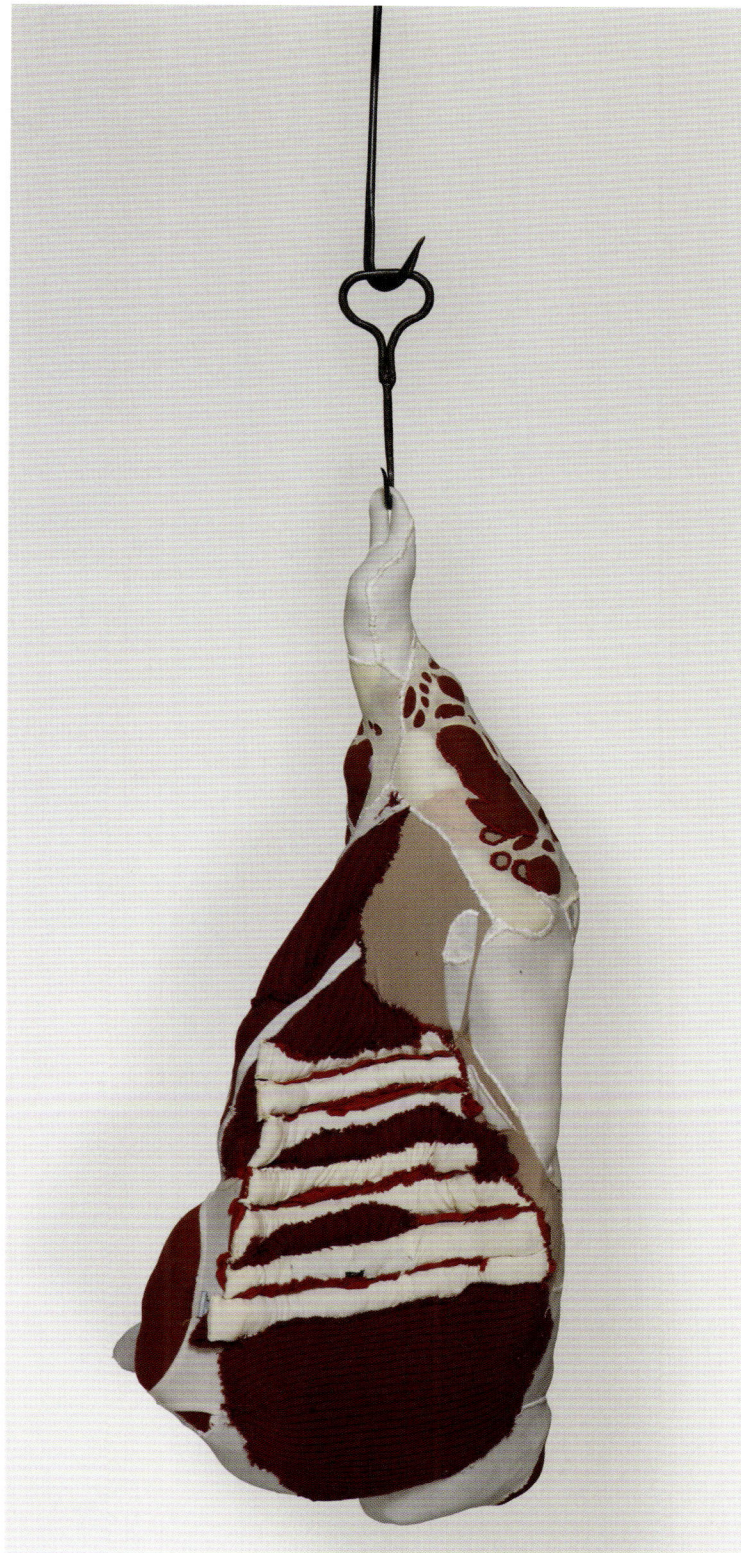

Tamara Kostianovsky
Motherland (Tierra Madre)
2007
Artist's clothing, embroidery, floss batting
wire, meat hook
67 × 28 × 15 in. (170.2 × 71.1 × 38.1 cm)

Rosângela Rennó

Scar

1998

Cibachrome, mounted and laminated

65½ × 47 in. (166.4 × 119.4 cm)

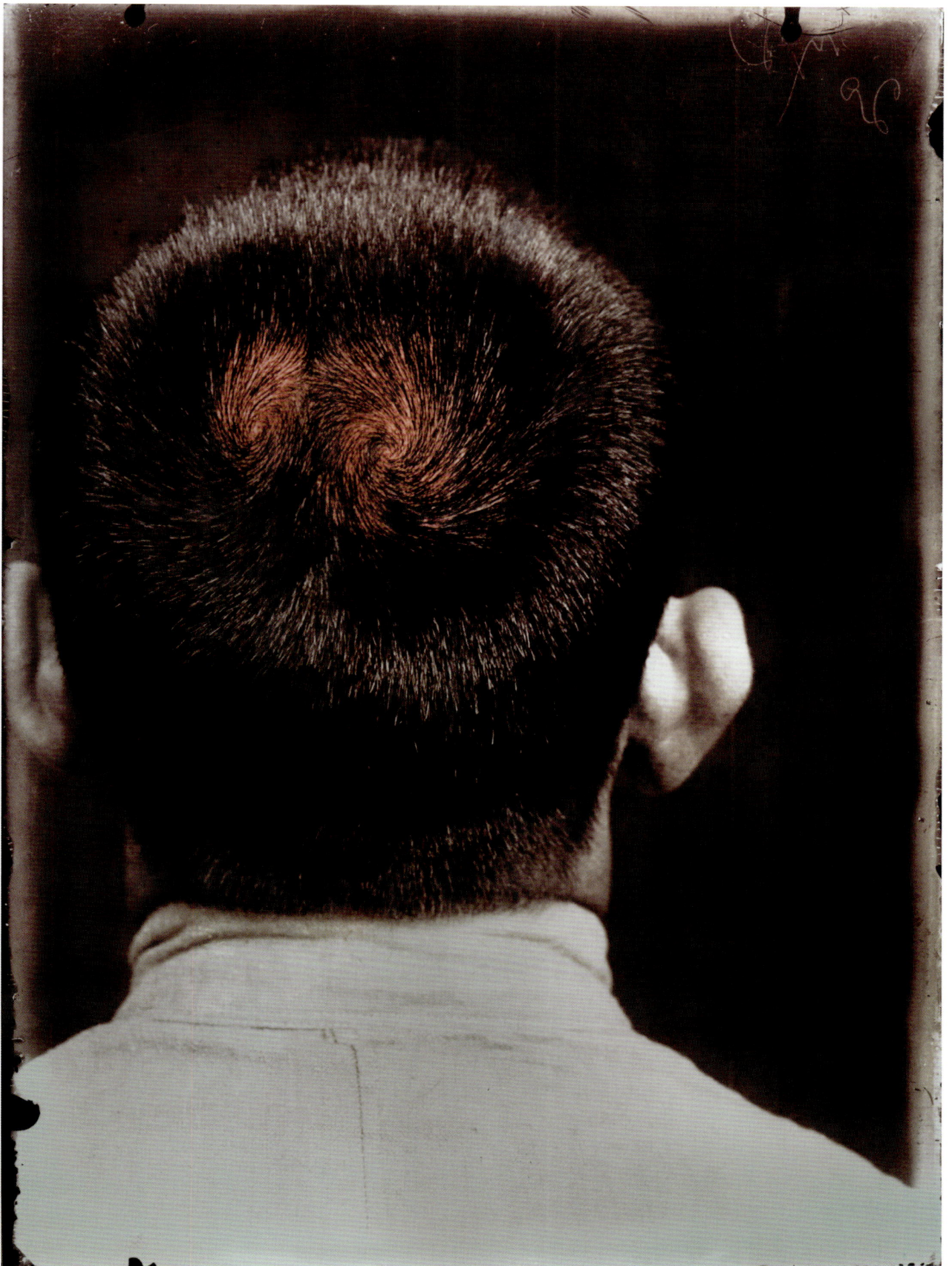

Rosângela Rennó
Double Crown
1998
Cibachrome, mounted and laminated
65½ × 47 in. (166.4 × 119.4 cm)

Tim White-Sobieski
Lab Party from the series *Before They Were
Beatles*
2006
Chromogenic print
71¾ × 86⅝ in. (182.1 × 220 cm)

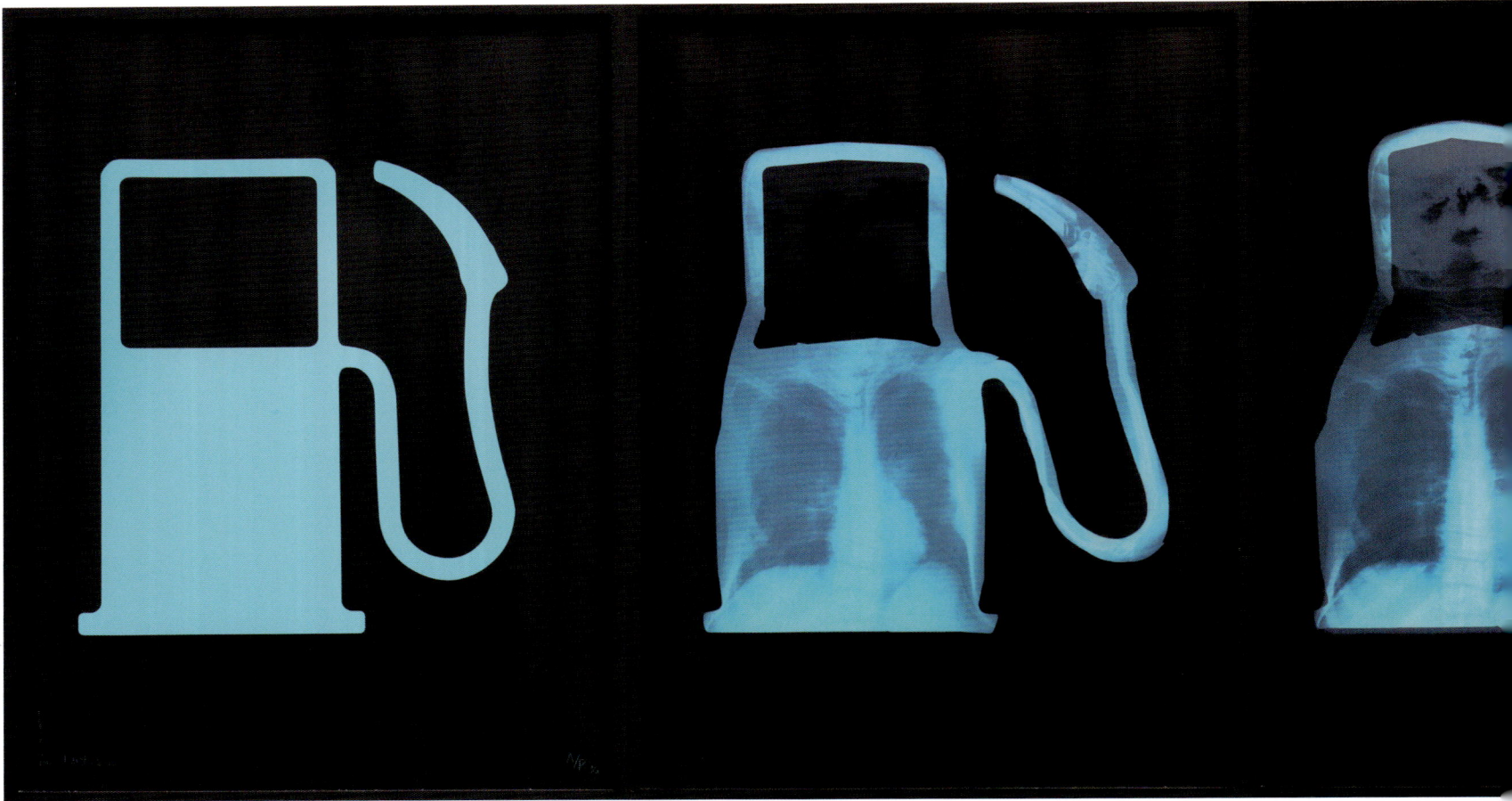

Ahmed Mater

Evolution of Man

2010

Five silkscreens in color

Each 31½ × 23½ in. (80 × 59.7 cm)

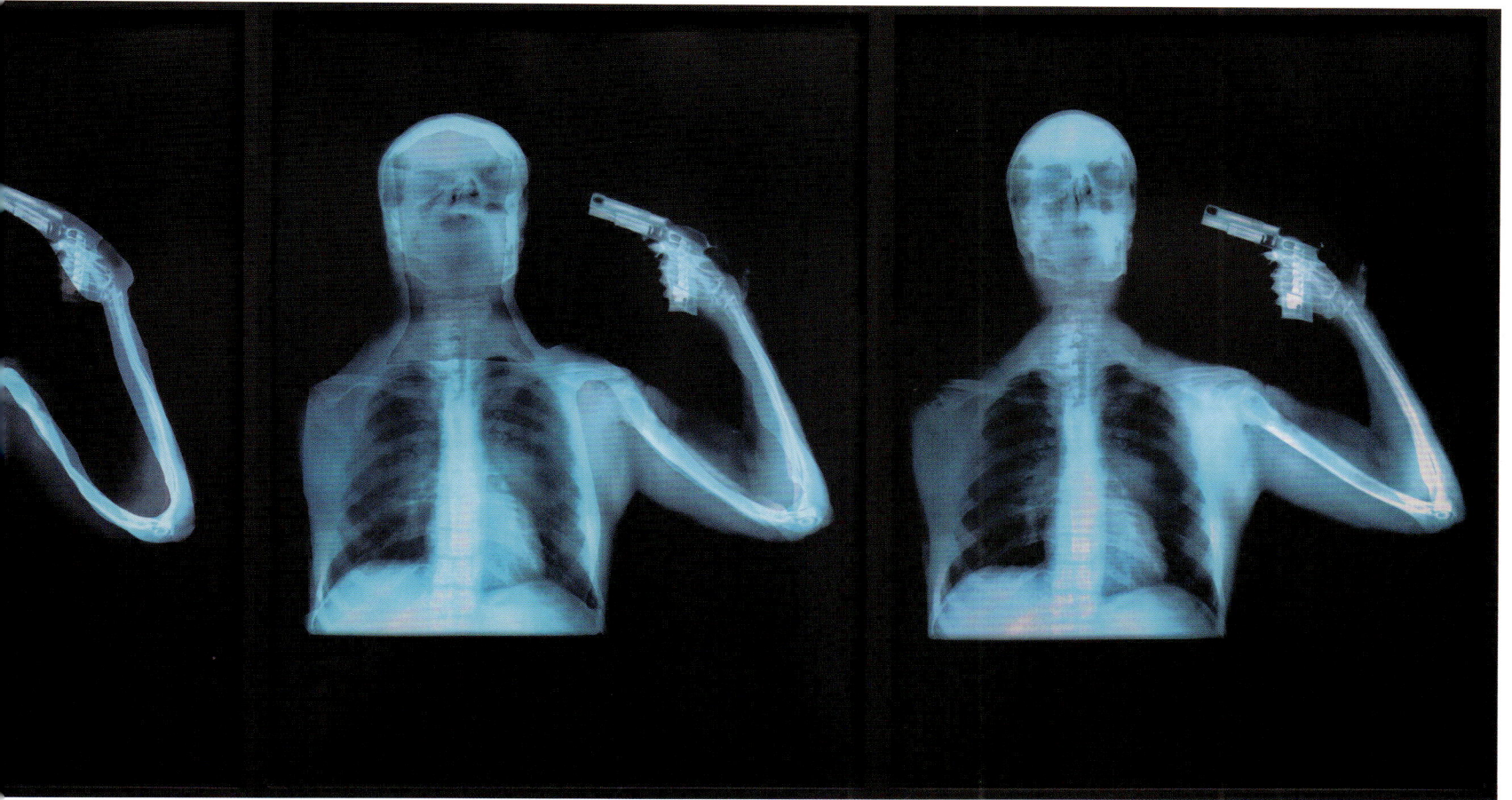

KITCHEN, HALL, STAIRS, BALCONY

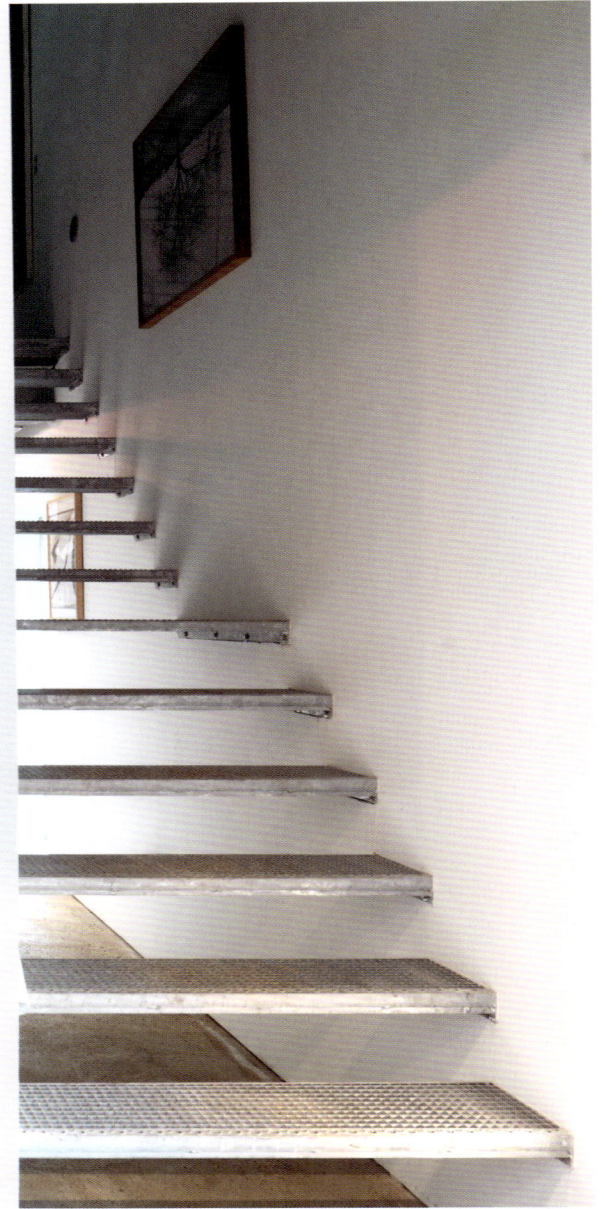

Naoki Koide

A Couple

2004

FRP, acrylic, lacquer, urethane

Woman: 64⅝ × 12⅝ × 1 in. (164.1 × 32 × 2.5 cm)

Man: 45 × 22 × 15 in. (114.3 × 55.9 × 38.1 cm)

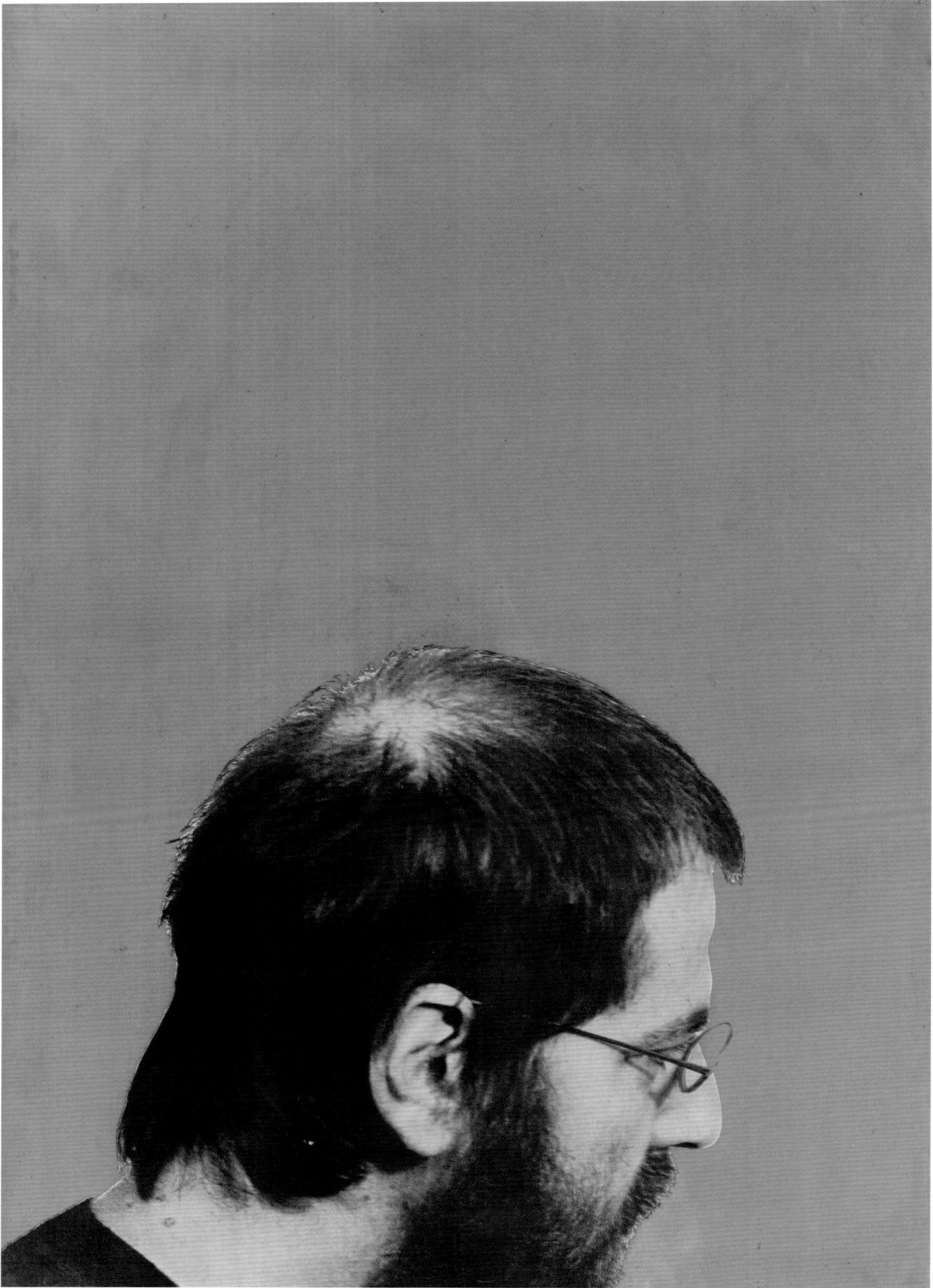

Michelangelo Pistoletto
Self-Portrait
1970
Silkscreen print on polished stainless steel
19¾ × 13¾ in. (50.2 × 34.9 cm)

Yannick Demmerle
Sans titre
2002
C-print, Diasec on aluminum
59¼ × 78¾ in. (150.2 × 200 cm)

Donald Judd
Untitled
1971
Galvanized iron
4 × 27 × 23 in. (10.2 × 68.6 × 58.4 cm)

Jennifer Allora & Guillermo Calzadilla

U.N. Top Burner

2005

Laser-cut steel, single-burner hot plate

10 × 8¾ × 4 in. (25.4 × 22.2 × 10.2 cm)

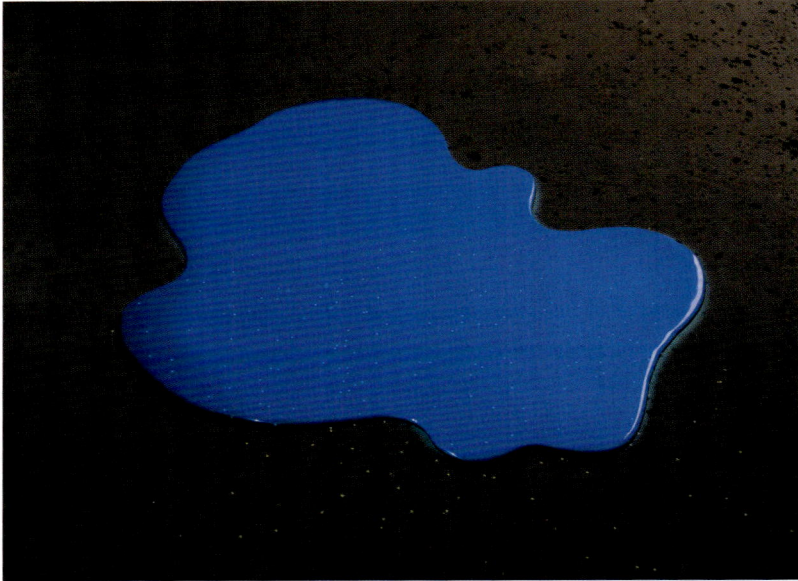

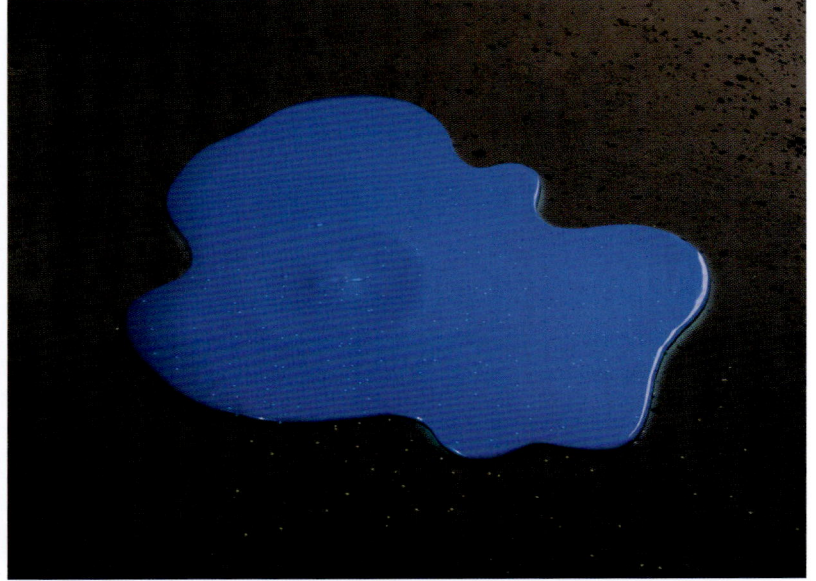

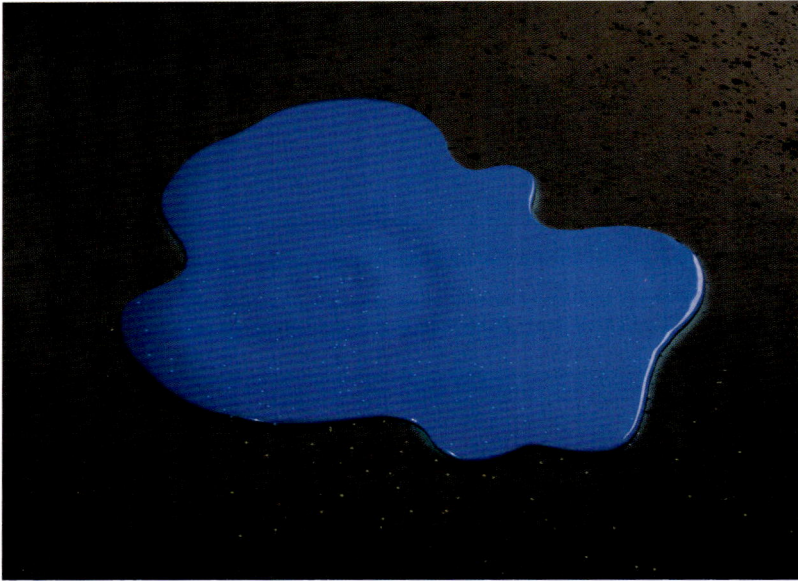

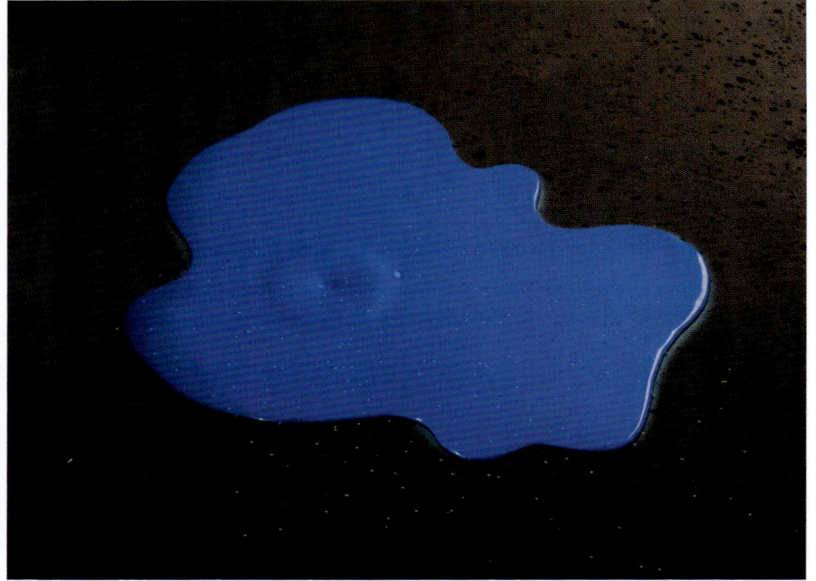

Peter Sarkisian

Blue Puddle 8

2002

Tinted polymer resin on masonite,
video, audio

Dimensions variable

Sylvie Fleury

Slim-Fast

1993

Serigraph on ten wood blocks

Each 18 × 15 × 10 in. (45.7 × 38.1 ×
25.4 cm)

Wang Jin

Ice 96, Central China

1996

Two black and white photographs

Each 30⅜ × 45¼ in. (77.2 × 114.9 cm) or

the reverse

Jörg Sasse
5610
2004
C-print
66⅞ × 57 in. (169.9 × 145 cm)

Gregor Zivic
Untitled
1998
C-print on aluminum
12 × 16 in. (30.5 × 40.6 cm)

Sigmar Polke
Ohne Titel (Working Drawing)
1968
Black and white photograph
40 × 37¼ in. (101.6 × 94.6 cm)

Arnold Odermatt
18 Car Crash Photos from Switzerland
from the series *Karambolage*
1959–79
Black and white photographs
11¾ × 15¾ in. (29.8 × 40 cm)

Anna & Bernhard Blume

Gebet im Wald (Forest Prayer), from the series *Im Wald (In the Forest)*

1990–91

Black and white photographs (sequence of three)

Each 8½ × 5⅞ in. (15 × 21.6 cm)

Anna & Bernhard Blume
Kontakt mit Bäumen (Contact with Trees), from the series
Im Wald (In the Forest)
1987–90
Black and white photographs (sequence of three)
Each 9⅞ × 6⅞ in. (24.8 × 17.5 cm)

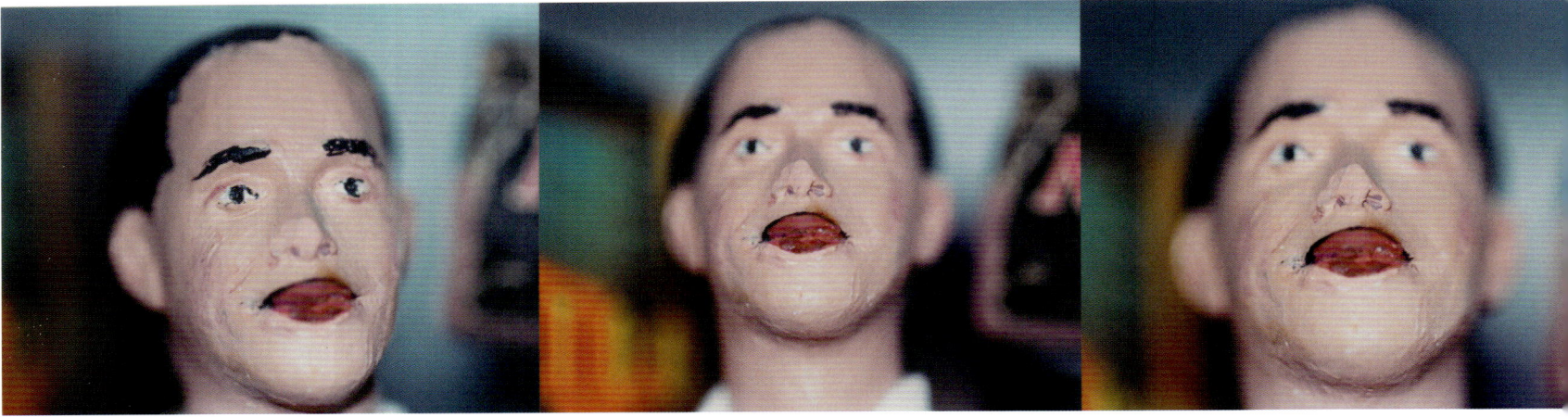

John Waters

Self Portrait No. 2
2000
Five c-prints
Each 8 × 10 in (20.3 × 25.4 cm)

John Waters

Self Portrait No. 3
2003
Felt-tip pen, pushpins, cut and pasted
gelatin silver print, synthetic polymer
paint, toy cockroaches, stamped ink,
transfer type, and pressure sensitive
tape on gelatin silver print and C-print,
in eight parts
14 × 56 in. (35.6 × 142.2 cm)

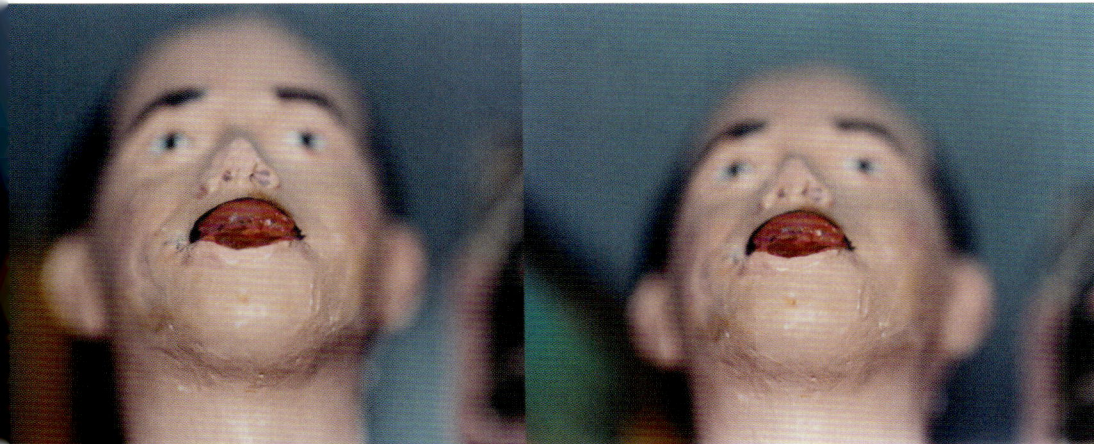

Gregor Zivic
Untitled
1998
C-print on aluminum
41 × 50 in. (104.1 × 127 cm)

Axel Lieber
Short Cuts
2005
Painted wood
6.7 × 4.7 × 4.9 in. (17 × 11.9 × 12.4 cm)

Kim Jones
Untitled (Doll)
2004–11
Plastic doll, wood, acrylic, ink, cord
28 × 17 × 14 in. (71.1 × 43.2 × 35.6 cm)

Rodney Graham
Oak Trees, Red Bluff (2)
1993
Silver gelatin print
30 × 39 in. (76.2 × 99.1 cm)

Kim Jones

Rat Box
2004–10
Wood, rubber rats, acrylic, ink
14 ½ × 20 × 8 in. (36.6 × 50.8 × 20.3 cm)

Loretta Lux
Maria 1
2001
Ilfochrome print
11¾ × 11¾ in. (29.8 × 29.8 cm)

Maria 2
2001
Ilfochrome print
11¾ × 11¾ in. (29.8 × 29.8 cm)

Huang Yong Ping

Amerigo Vespucci
2003
Aluminum
29⅛ × 31½ × 51⅛ in. (73.9 × 80 × 130 cm)

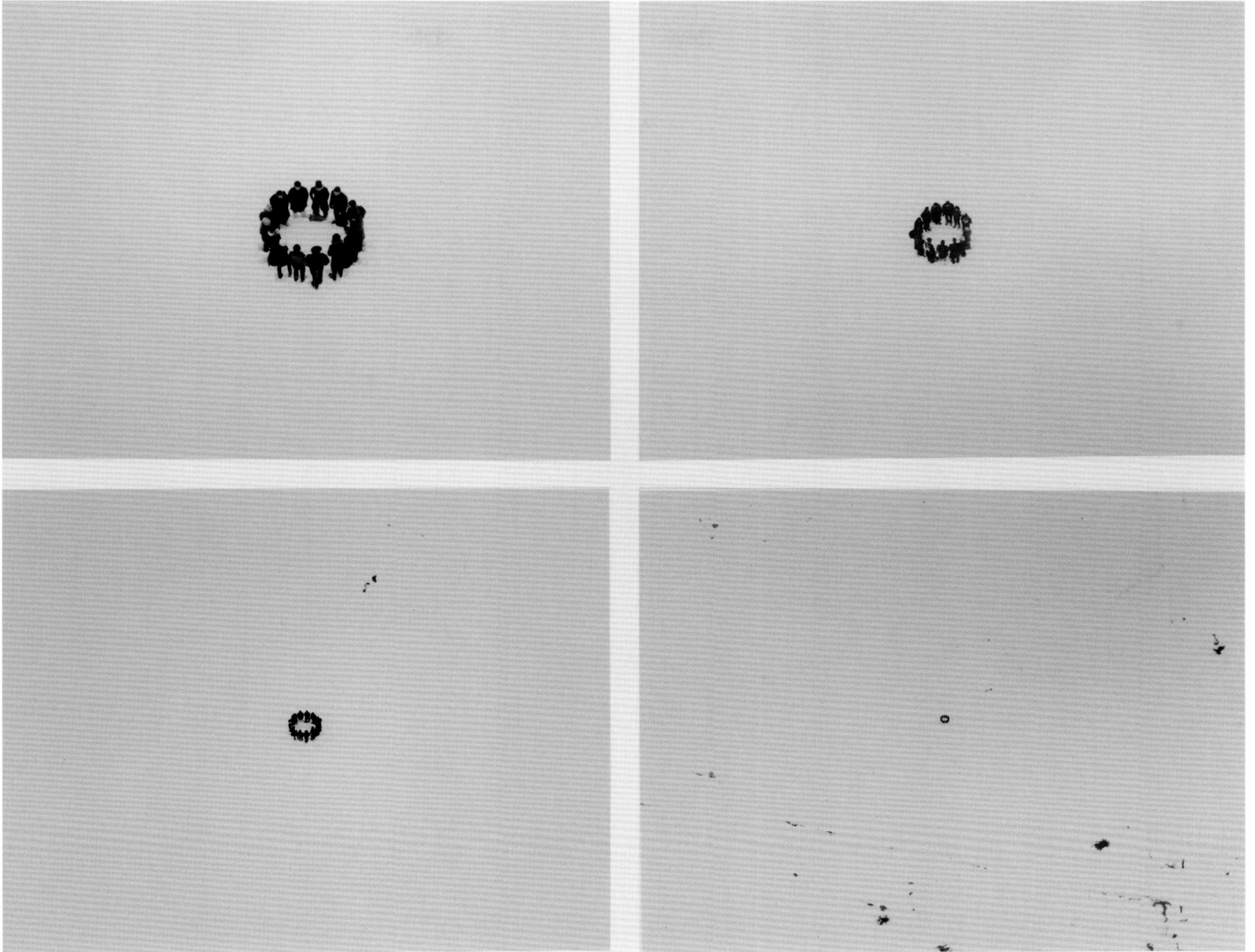

Doug Aitken
Conspiracy
1998
C-print mounted on plexiglass
48 × 48 in. (121.9 × 121.9 cm)

PAGES 200–201

Asta Gröting
Convention/ces poupées qui disent oui
2000
Black and white photograph
49⅛ × 86⅝ in. (120 × 220 cm)

EAST
GALLERY

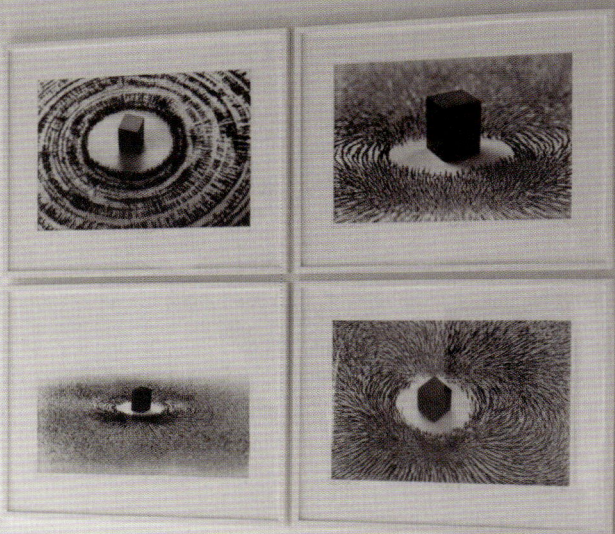

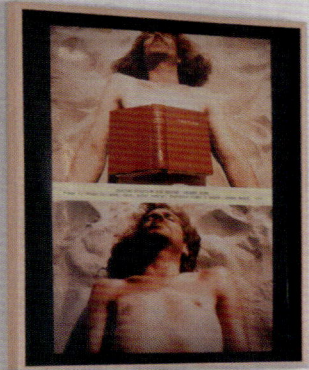

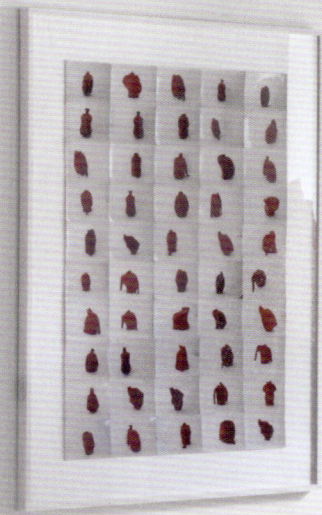

ABOVE

Frederick Kiesler

Galaxy A

1961

Pastel on paper and wood construction

67¾ × 36 × 15 in. (172.1 × 91.4 × 38.1 cm)

FACING PAGE

Yinka Shonibare

Leisure Lady (with Pugs)

2001

Three fiberglass dogs, Dutch wax-printed
cloth, mannequin

160 × 80 × 80 in. (406.4 × 203.2 × 203.2 cm)

Wolfgang Laib

Milkstone
1992–95
White marble, milk
2¼ × 20½ × 24⅜ in. (6 × 52 × 62 cm)

Alan Saret

ING

1983

Wire

48½ × 60 × 40 in. (123.2 × 152.4 × 101.6 cm)

Asta Gröting

Space Between Lovers / Unfolded
2008
Silicone
9 × 24 ⅜ × 56 ¾ in. (23 × 62 × 144.1 cm)

Dennis Oppenheim

Reading Position for Second Degree Burn
1970
C-print
20 × 24 in. (50.8 × 61 cm)

READING POSITION FOR SECOND   DEGREE BURN
Stage I, Stage II. Book, skin, solar energy. Exposure time: 5 hours. Jones Beach. 1970

Anish Kapoor
Untitled Nos. 17, 18, 20, 21 (Gourds)
1995–99
Acrylic pigment, gourds, in four parts
Dimensions variable

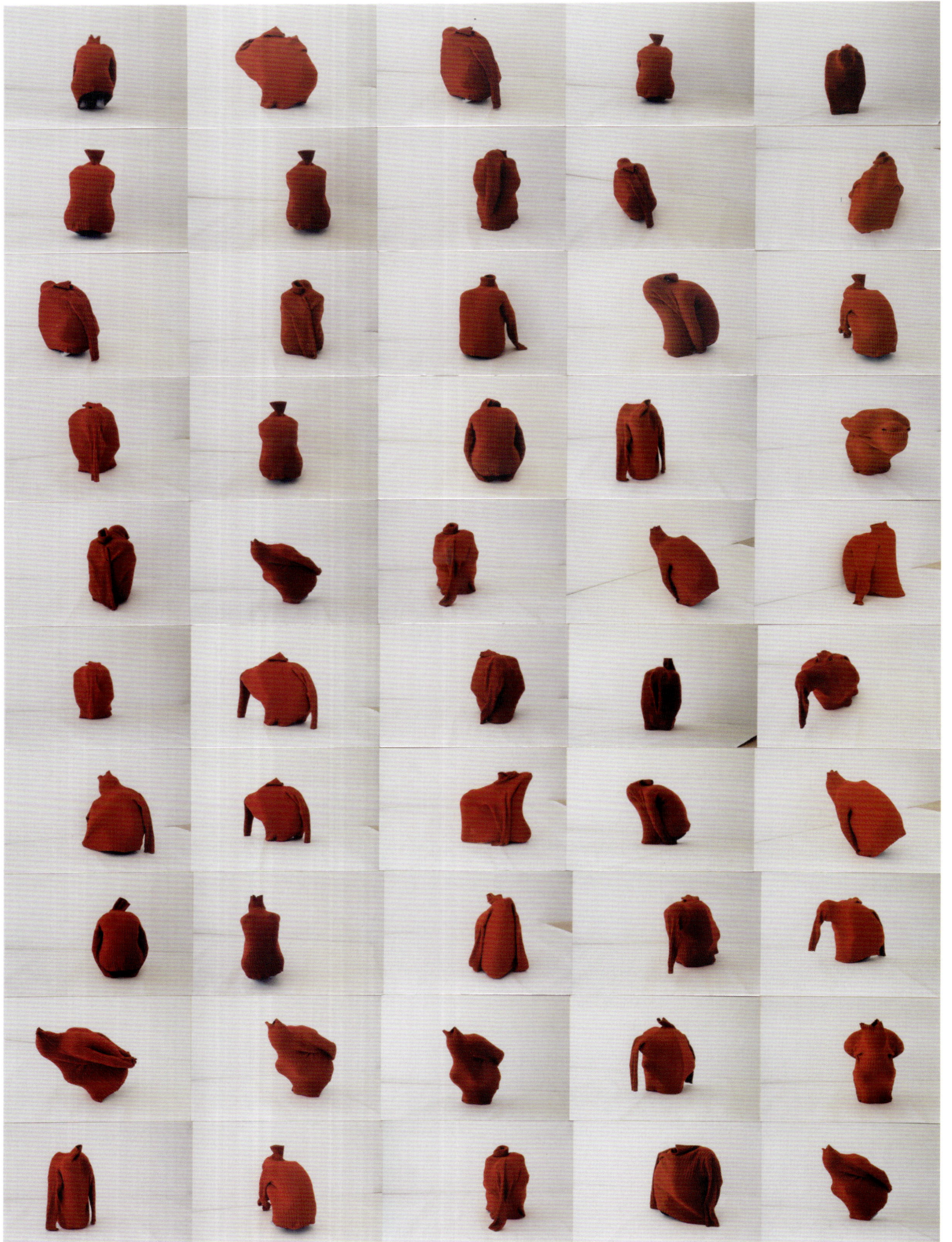

ABOVE

Christoph Büchel
Parade
2005
DVD, color, sound
9 minutes, 36 seconds

FACING PAGE

Erwin Wurm
Untitled (Red Sweaters / One Minute Sculptures)
2000
Photo collage on cardboard
40 × 28 in. (101.6 × 71.1 cm)

Moyra Davey & Jason Simon
E-Bay (1–30), *E-Bay (31–60)*, *E-Bay (61–91)*
2000
Three C-prints
Each 40 × 44¼ in. (101.6 × 112.4 cm)

Roman Signer
Aktion auf der Steinach
1991
C-print, aluminum, in five parts
Each 13 ½ × 20 in. (34.3 × 50.8 cm)

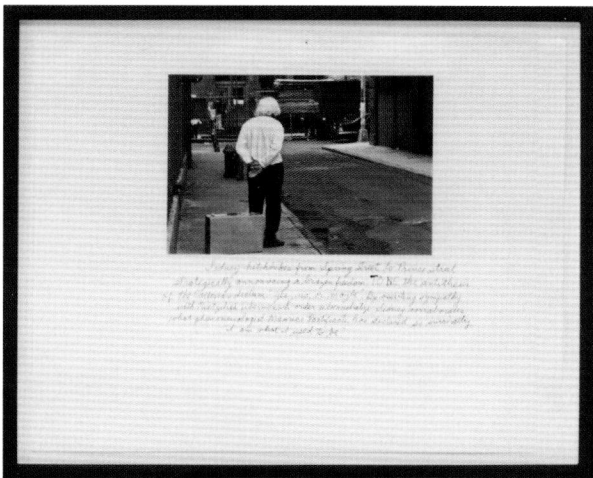

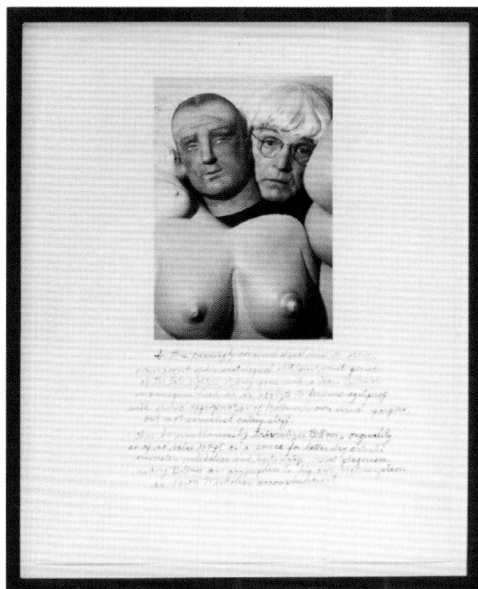

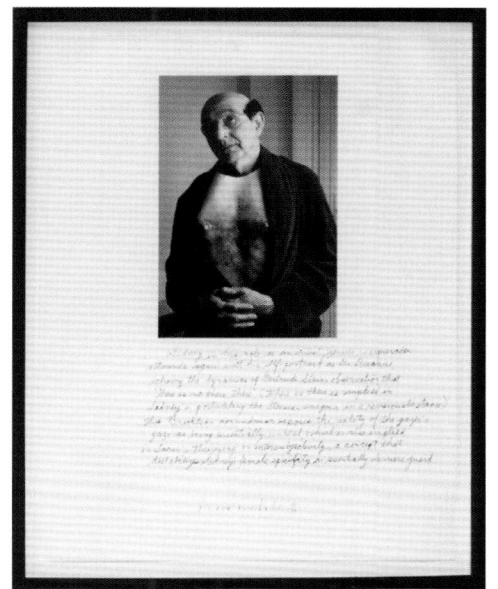

Duane Michals

Who is Sidney Sherman?

2000

Six gelatin silver prints with hand-applied text

Each 4¾ × 7 in. (12.1 × 17.8 cm)

Bae Bien-U
SNM1A-006H from the series *Sonamu*
2002
C-print
52¾ × 102 in. (134.1 × 259.1 cm)

Rosemary Laing

Brownwork No. 9

1999

C-print

40 × 60 in. (101.6 × 152.4 cm)

Carlos Garaicoa
Untitled
2003
Black and white photograph, thread, pins
68⅞ × 48⅛ in. (175 × 122.4 cm)

WEST GALLERY

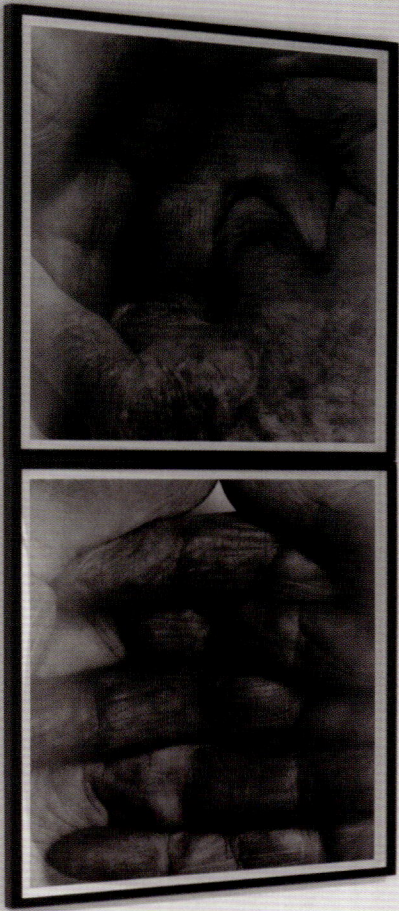

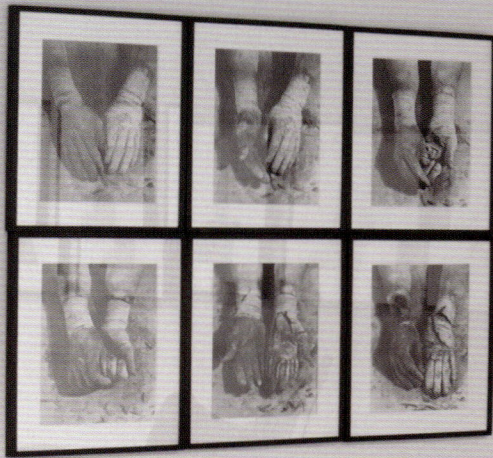

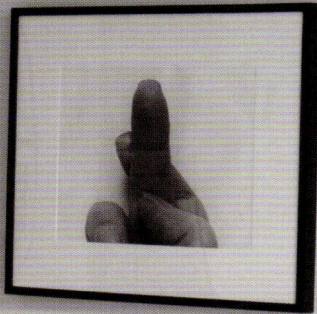

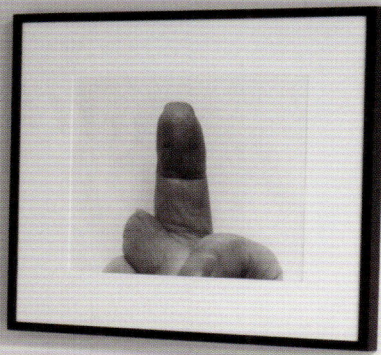

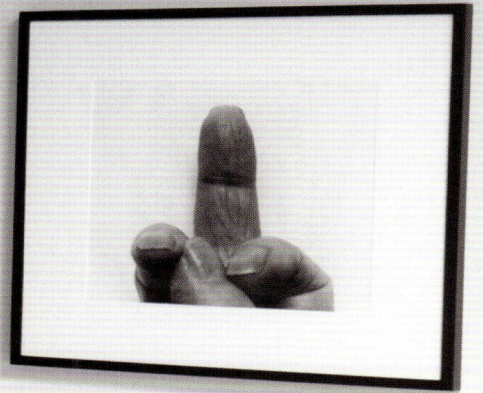

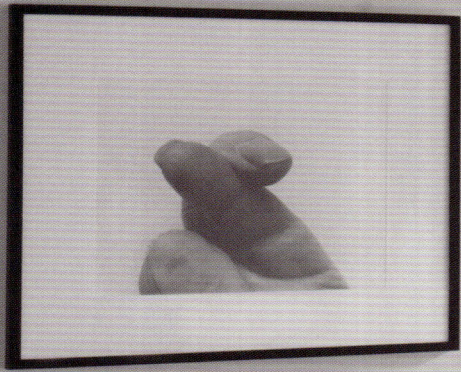

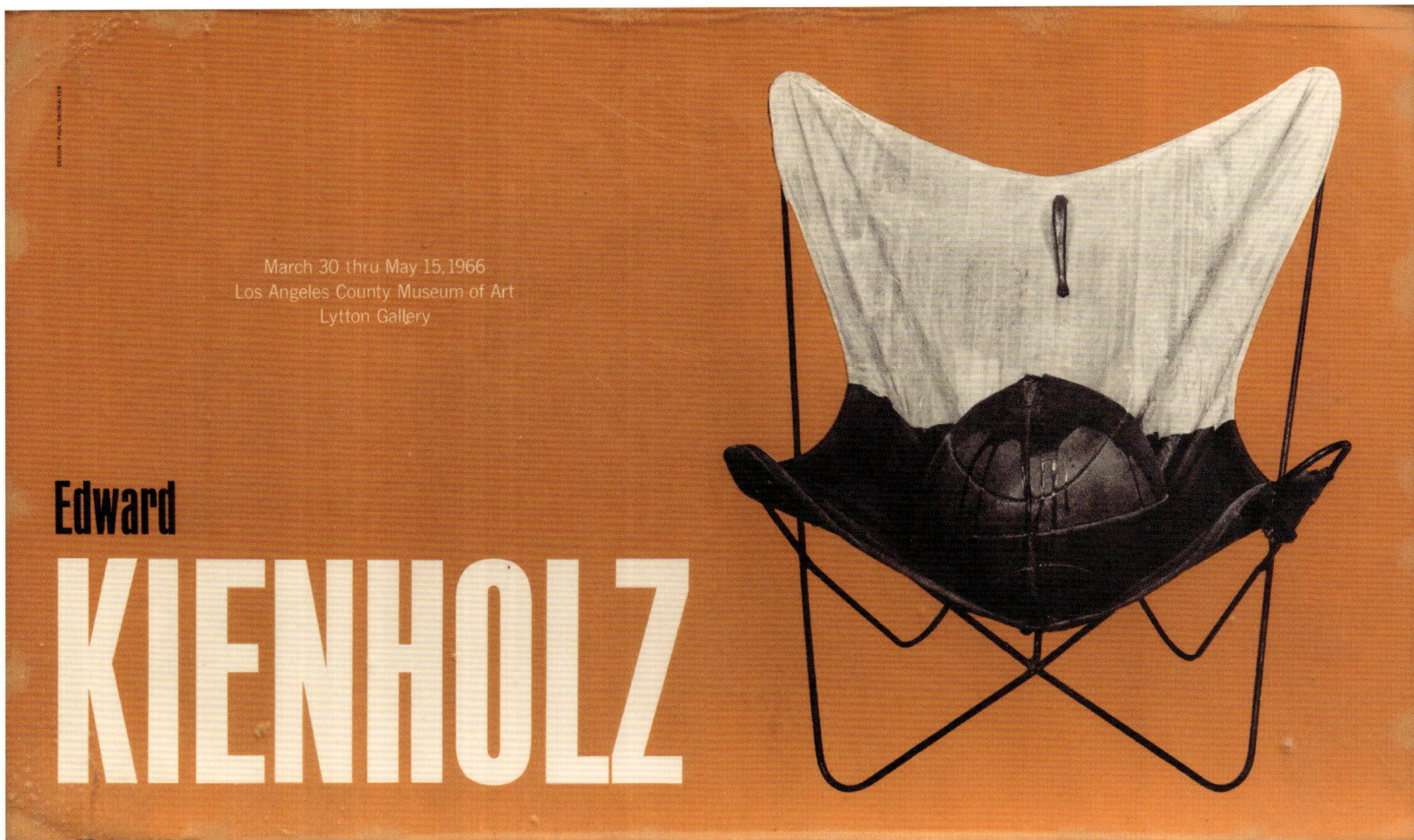

ABOVE

Edward Kienholz

"Edward Kienholz" Los Angeles County
Museum of Art Exhibition Poster
1966
Offset Lithograph

FACING PAGE

Edward Kienholz

I'm Not a Fig-Plucker, Nor a Fig-Plucker's Son,
but I'll Pluck Your Figs 'til a Fig-Plucker Comes
1963
Canvas chair, medicine ball, resin, brown
tape, metal door handle
38¼ × 34½ × 30½ in. (97.2 × 87.6 × 77.5 cm)

Edward Kienholz

Drawing for State Hospital

1966

Relief construction with ink and graphite
on paper with varnish, laid down on
clipboard in wood box with metal bars

23 × 17 × 4½ in. (58.4 × 43.2 × 11.4 cm)

Edward Kienholz

Moses

1959

Wagon, doll heads, glass jar, acrylic,
wood, metal

24 × 42 × 11¾ in. (61 × 106.7 × 29.8 cm)

FACING PAGE

Erik Schmidt
There's Enough to Go Around
2012
Oil on canvas
86⅝ × 59 in. (220 × 150 cm)

ABOVE

Natasja Kensmil
La Danse Macabre
2007
Oil on linen
78¾ × 78¾ in. (199.9 × 199.9 cm)

Katrin Sigurdardóttir

Untitled

2006

Plywood, polystyrene, resin, paint,
hardware, transit labels
Dimensions variable, approx. 30 × 40 × 10 in.
(76 × 102 × 25 cm)

Wangechi Mutu

Throne

2006

Wood chair, wood, leather, wine, glass
bottle, rubber stopper
110 × 45 × 36 in. (279.4 × 114.3 × 91.4 cm)

Georges Rousse

Drewen
2009
C-print on aluminum
70⅞ × 98⅜ in. (180 × 250 cm)

Georges Rousse

Athene

1993

C-print on aluminum

63 × 49¼ in. (160 × 125 cm)

Candida Höfer
Festspielhaus Recklinghausen VII 1997
1997
C-print
47¼ × 47½ in. (120 × 120.7 cm)

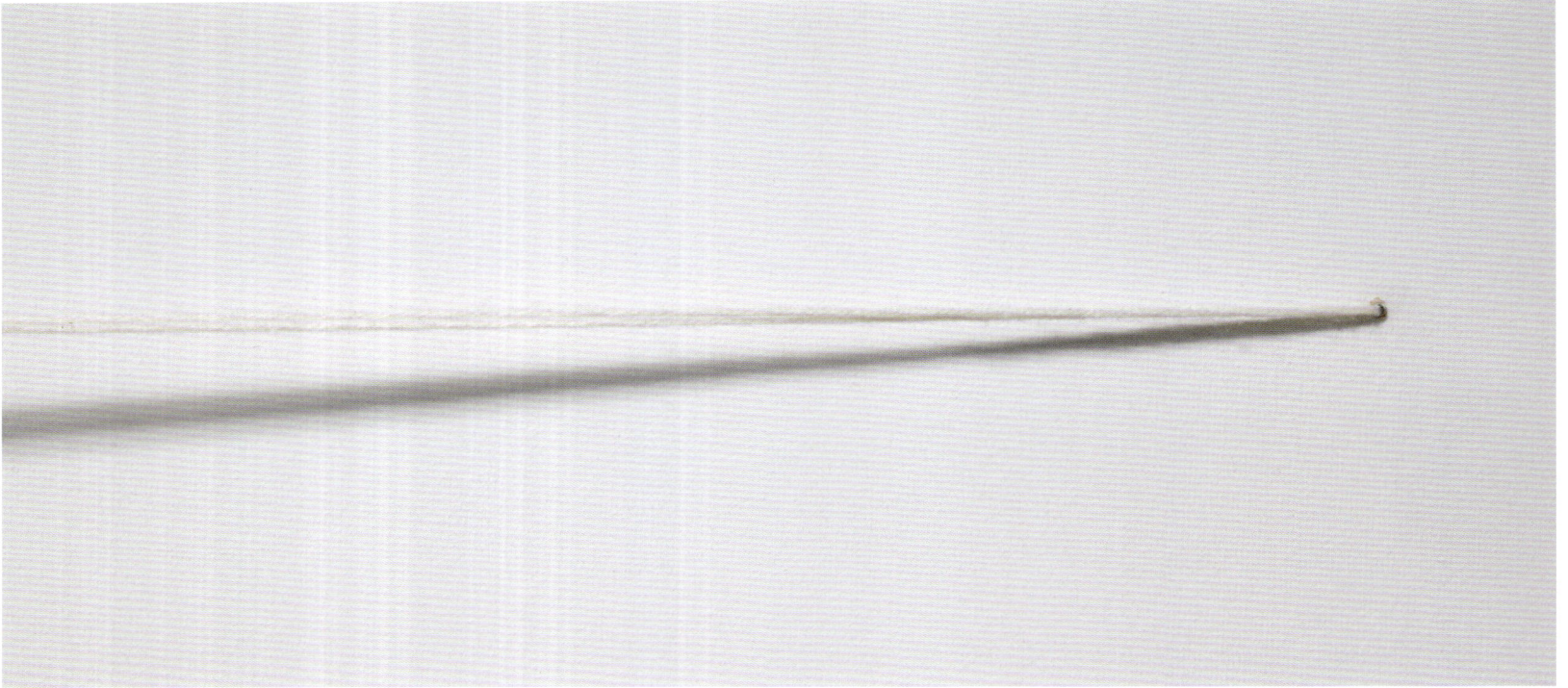

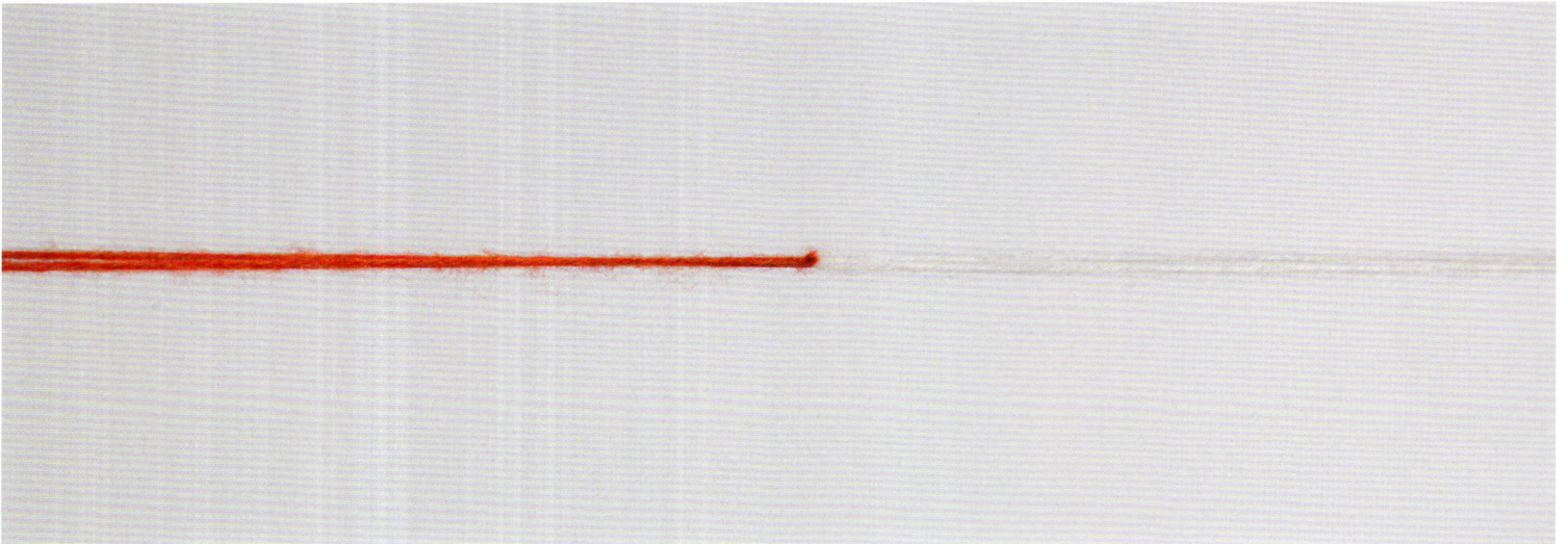

Fred Sandback

Untitled

1987

Cardinal red and white acrylic yarn, three strands

62 × 12 × 138 in. (157.5 × 30.5 × 350.5 cm)

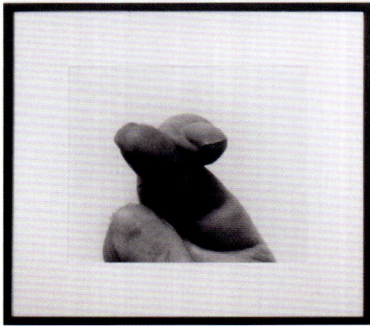

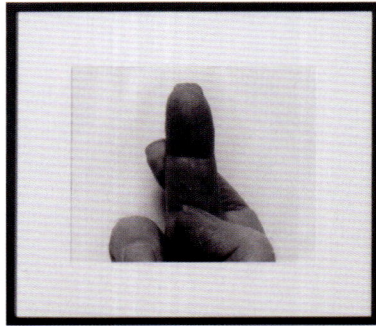

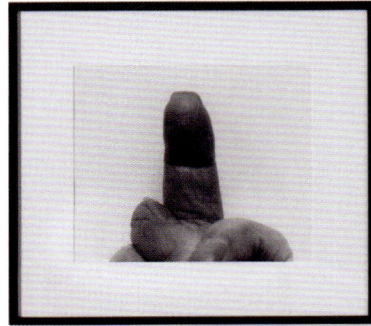

John Coplans
Crossed Fingers (Nos. 1–7), 1999
1999
Seven gelatin silver prints
Each 17¼ × 20½ in. (43.8 × 52.1 cm)

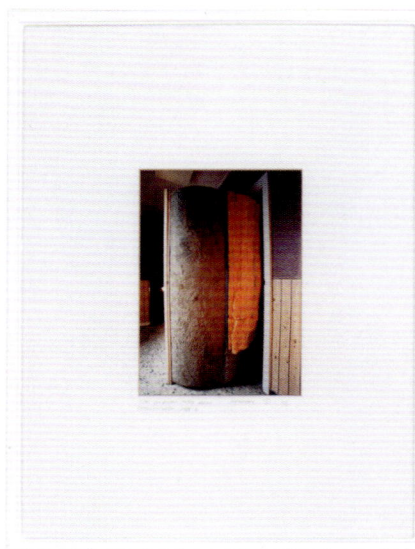

Gregor Schneider
Giesenkirchen
1989–91
Eight C-prints
Each 7 × 5 in. (17.8 × 12.7 cm)

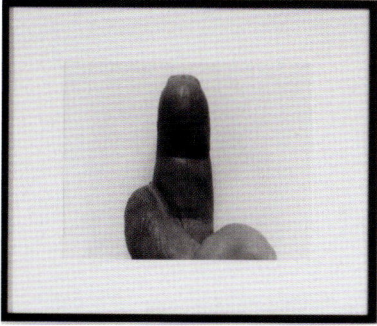 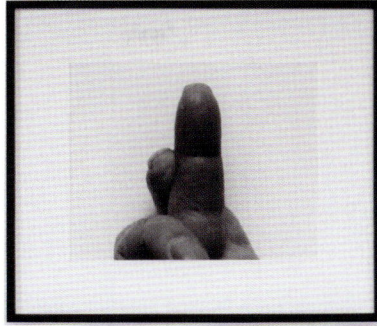 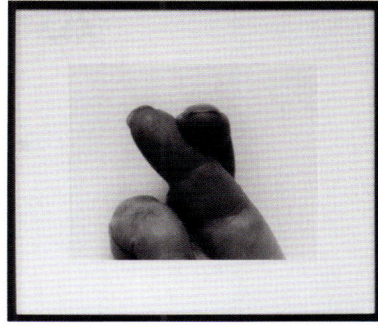

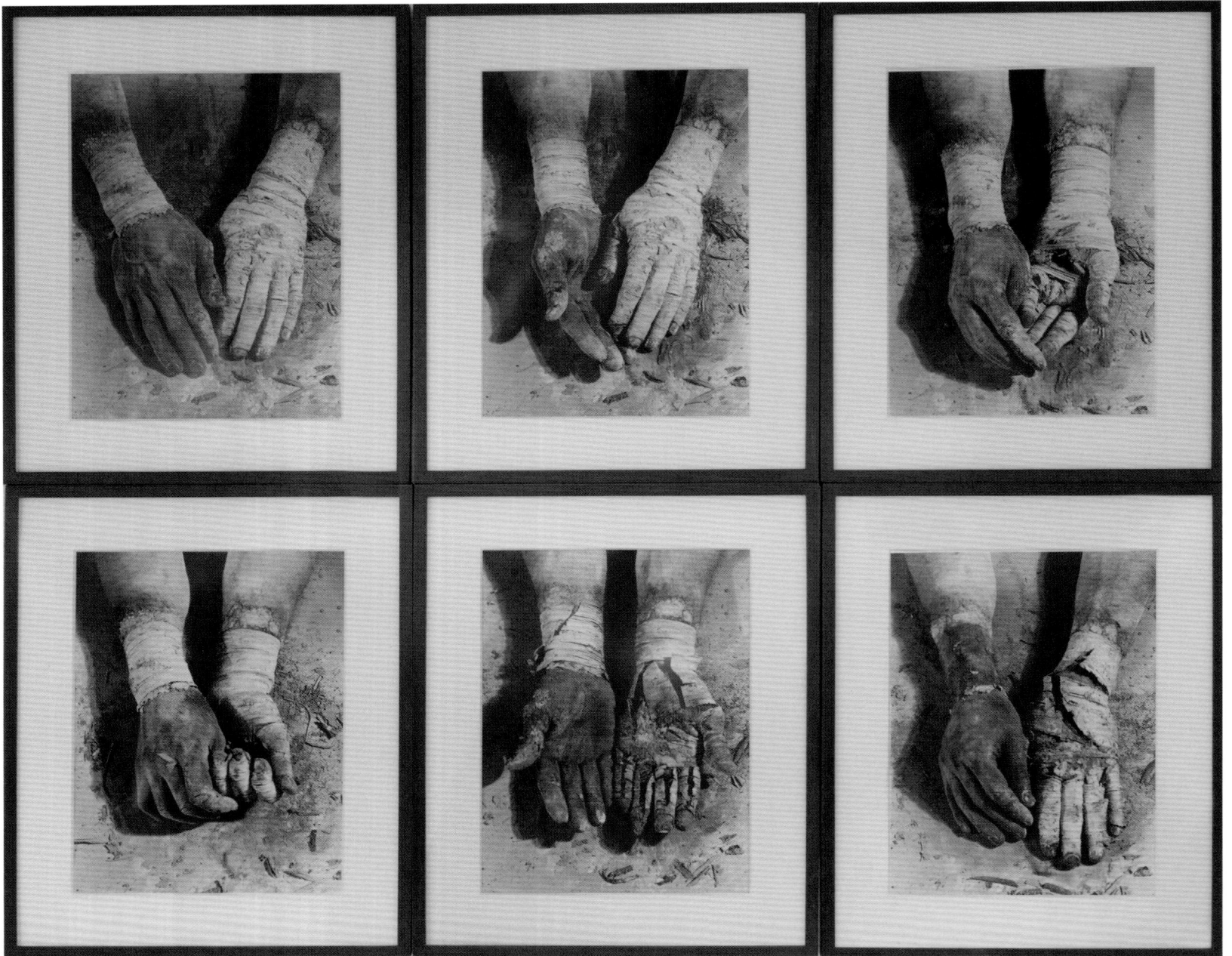

Dieter Appelt

Die Befreiung der Finger
1979
Six gelatin silver prints
Each 15¾ × 11¾ in. (39.9 × 30 cm)

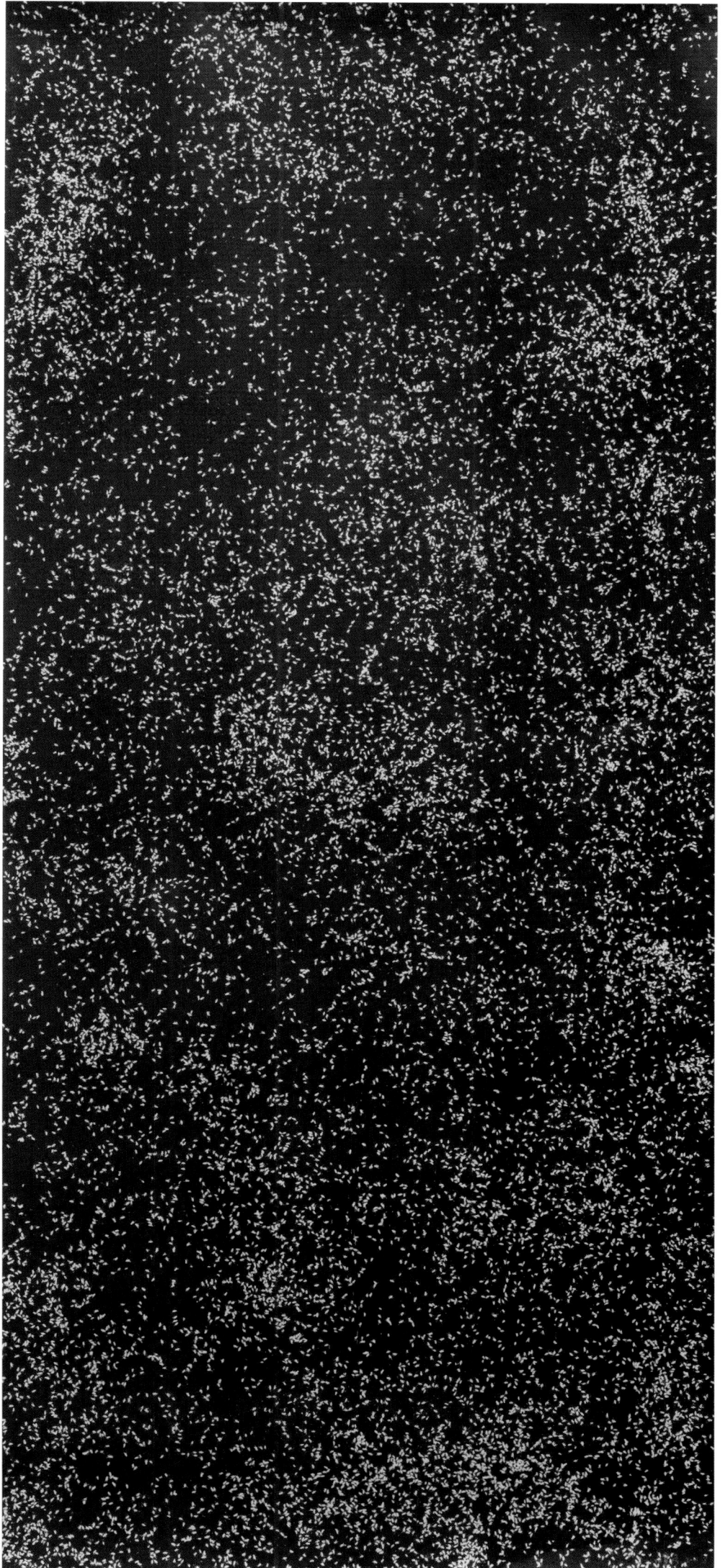

Bai Yiluo
Flies II
2001
Photogram
90⅓ × 40⅛ in. (229.9 × 201.1 cm)

OUTDOOR SCULPTURE

ART IN THE WOODS

by Walter Robinson

It turns out I have a soft spot for art in the woods. Not those big sculptures plopped down on the lawn at your typical sculpture park or museum, all nice and bucolic but basically boring. I mean art that is *really* hidden away among the shrubs and the trees. I discovered this whimsical inclination of mine only in 2007, when the Romanian-born artist Serge Spitzer lured me out on a day trip to a densely wooded, seventeen-acre plot on Quantuck Bay in Quiogue, New York.

He was characteristically mysterious about our destination, but I was an art journalist, and when an artist beckoned, my inclination was to follow. Serge did tip me off that the place belonged to one Jerome Stern, then 84, who I later found out was a trustee of the New Museum, a patron of the Israel Museum, and a member of the photo committee at the Guggenheim Museum. He was also a voracious collector with decidedly unconventional tastes—in short, a player.

Spitzer had designed the building in 1997, a strikingly spare modernist structure, two stories encompassing 7,500 square feet and modestly dubbed the "ArtBarn." But the visit didn't begin at the ArtBarn—that was to be the climax of our visit. Instead, we started in the woods at the edge of the property, setting off on a path-free quest for artworks that could be spotted here and there among the trees.

Ever cosmopolitan, art has always turned to nature for its model and ideal. The global environmentalism of the 1960s developed in tandem with earthworks and a range of nature art. In the New York art scene of the '90s, however, contemporary art took a less optimistic course, embracing the abject and the downtrodden with a vengeance. Art might still be good for you, but largely as an object lesson. Several of the works installed in the woods at the ArtBarn have this abject cast. They are not so much appealing or harmonious as jarring. They upset their woodland setting, as if to comment not on our unity with nature but rather our estrangement from it.

A case in point is the bronze fountain by Swedish artist Ann-Sofi Sidén, a life-size self-portrait cast that depicts the artist squatting, pants lowered around her ankles, peeing. The situation is commonplace—surely everyone relieves themselves in the woods sometime in their lives—and yet a resolutely private one. The siting of the work where it is meant to be seen (I think of a similar pose captured in the 1980s by photographer Nan Goldin, who shot the writer Cookie Mueller, in full night-out makeup, skirt hiked up, doing her business in a downtown Manhattan alley) suggests a sensibility that has cast off what are thought to be trivial social conventions, though not without a certain air of weariness. Another level of defiance is indicated by Sidén's title for the work—*Fideicommissum*—which refers to the centuries-old Swedish law by which the landed gentry passed their property intact to a male heir. *Fideicommissum* was originally commissioned in 2000 for the grounds of a park at a castle in Sweden. Here, sheltered in a nook formed by some bushes, the sculpture is a particularly feminist take on the conventional pastoral fountain, and certainly far more starkly realistic than those precedents.

Given its placement among other artworks in nature, Sidén's fountain also comments on artistic ego in general, implying that she is aggressively "marking her territory" as a wild animal would. In this respect, the work bears a tangential relationship to another sculpture we saw on the property that day, a life-size aluminum statue of a Neapolitan Mastiff by the Paris-based Chinese artist Huang Yong Ping. The dog lifts one leg to relieve itself, creating a silvery puddle in the shape of the United States. The 2003 work is named *Amerigo Vespucci*, a nod to the Italian explorer whose voyages contributed to the competition by European powers to mark their territories in the New World.

The primal theme of relieving oneself in nature is also referenced by David Hammons's punningly titled *Toilet Tree* of 2004. An off-the-shelf commercial urinal strapped to the trunk of a pine tree, the work looks rather like a bit of human detritus that was somehow turned into a Duchampian readymade, perhaps through the intervention of a gang of insolent teenagers. *Toilet Tree* is a noble addition to the anti-art heritage of R. Mutt, Duchamp's alter ego. As a former Boy Scout who spent a fair amount of time camping outdoors,

I can testify personally to a special kind of cultural resonance that attends the discovery of such traces of trash civilization in the middle of otherwise pristine nature. Hammons's urinal conjures up exactly those woodland dumps where country folk dispose of old bedsprings and washing machines, or where young lovers hold their drunken rendezvous. Ecologically speaking, it's the Hudson River School turned on its twenty first-century head.

A work by the New York artist Nate Lowman restores a sense of the pastoral to the verdant grove, though in an ironical way. Lowman has had his own gravestone crafted, and it sits in a small, shaded clearing beneath the trees. Cemeteries are a primordial sculpture site, of course, as death is a primordial theme. But Lowman's sensibility can hardly be called somber—he is one of the New York art youthquake's more animated nihilists—and so his gravestone is a joke. It reads "HERE LIES NATE LOWMAN, VICTIM OF IDENTITY THEFT," the lines separated by the dates Feb. 1, 1979 – Dec. 7, 2006. The classical granite marker of mortality and remembrance has been reformulated as an upside-down comment on the ever au courant preoccupation with artistic originality and influence.

An entirely different response to the Arcadian site is embodied in Menashe Kadishman's lyrically titled *Necklace in the Forest*, an installation of twenty ochre-colored aluminum panels attached to the trunks of pine trees several feet above the forest floor, which here is covered by a dense layer of pine needles. Kadishman, who lived and worked in Tel Aviv and exhibited in the Israel pavilion at the 1978 Venice Biennale, presented an earlier version of the piece in a 1970 exhibition at the Jewish Museum in New York. On that occasion the golden rectangles were attached to trees in Central Park along Fifth Avenue, an intervention that preceded Christo and Jeanne-Claude's celebrated *Gates* (proposed in 1979 and installed in Central Park in 2005) and drew its own early outcry from park preservationists.

Later known for expressionistic sculptures cut by torch from sheet steel (his *Shalechet*, or "Fallen Leaves," a collection of hundreds of coin-like metal faces strewn upon the floor, is a favorite attraction

at the Jewish Museum, Berlin), Kadishman was a Minimalist in the 1960s and '70s. He brought a bit of illusionism to his blocky sculptures by suspending them in mid-air on sheets of glass. In the woods at the ArtBarn, the aluminum panels forge an uncanny bond between warm, breathing nature and a cool industrial aesthetic. This tension pervades the grounds with its range of sculptural subjects, materials, structures, and forms. There is a nude, life-size standing figure in cast iron by and of Antony Gormley, an over-scale painted cedar figure wearing an everyday white shirt and trousers by Stephan Balkenhol, three tall slit drums from Vanuatu in the Pacific, and a wooden Bembe house post and a stone monolith from Nigeria.

A post-apocalyptic element is introduced into the landscape by the nature-meets-technology artist Olafur Eliasson, whose *Spiral Tunnel*, designed for the property in 2001, is a kind of bower of spiraling stainless steel ribs rather than saplings and vines, its passage strewn not with rose petals but a rough, chunky gravel of black lava. More upbeat, with its implicit advocacy of creative recycling, is a large, freestanding pavilion by the German duo Wolfgang Winter and Berthold Horbelt. It is one of their trademark "Cratehouses," made of more than 800 stacked plastic water-bottle crates.

After traversing the wooded grounds, it was almost a surprise to come upon the ArtBarn itself, all but hidden by the surrounding trees. A simple structure covered with sheets of corrugated steel, the building had textured concrete floors, an asymmetrical concrete plaza (marked by a perforated stainless steel bench by Scott Burton), and steel walkways and terraces, all designed by Spitzer in a straightforward and cost-effective way. The name "ArtBarn" also serves as its own kind of camouflage: keeping this institution, and its sprawl of interconnected artworks both inside and out, nestled amongst the woods.

FACING PAGE

Marcos Ramírez Erre

Los ojos de la libertad miran hacia adentro (The Eyes of Freedom Look Within) #2

2000

Aluminum and plastic

144 in. (365.8 cm) high

ABOVE

David Hammons

Toilet Tree

2004

Ceramic urinal, rubber tube, plastic rope

259

Ann-Sofi Sidén

Fideicommissum
2000
Bronze fountain
39¼ × 19¾ × 18½ in. (99.8 × 50 × 47 cm)

ABOVE

Unidentified Artist (Nigeria)
Ejagham Monolith (Akwanshi)
From the Cross River region, Nigeria
Approx. 57 in. (144.8 cm) high

FACING PAGE

Unidentified Artist (Ethiopia)
Arussi Standing Male Figure
From the Jimma region, Ethiopia
Approx. 6 ft. (1.8 m) high

Stephan Balkenhol

Grosser Mann (Large Man)

1994

Painted cedar

88 × 39 × 22 in. (223.5 × 99.1 × 56 cm)

Nate Lowman

Nate Lowman

2006–7

Granite

44 × 44 × 12 in. (111.8 × 111.8 × 30.5 cm)

Unidentified Artist (Vanuatu)

Three Slit Gongs

From Ambrym

Each approx. 11 ft (3.4 m) to 17 ft (5.2 m) high

LEFT

Menashe Kadishman
Om
1969
Stainless steel
192 × 240 × 60 in. (487.7 × 609.6 × 152.4 cm)

PAGES 270–1

Menashe Kadishman
Necklace in the Forest
1970
Twenty aluminum panels affixed to trees
Each 72 × 36 in. (182.9 × 91.4 cm)

Menashe Kadishman
Five Dogs
2010
Bronze
Each approx. 30 in. (76.2 cm) high

Antony Gormley

Diaphragm III

1997

Cast iron

74 × 21¾ × 13¾ in. (188 × 55.2 × 34.9 cm)

FOREGROUND

Zadok Ben-David
Single Green Leaf
1988
Iron and colored cement
Approx. 16 ft. (4.9 m) high

BACKGROUND

High Noon
1988
Iron and colored cement
132 × 40 in. (335.3 × 101.6 cm)

ABOVE

Scott Burton
Bench
1998
Stainless steel
34 × 60 × 32 in. (86.4 × 152.4 × 81.3 cm)

Wolfgang Winter & Berthold Hörbelt

Cratehouse 843.13 (Pavilion)

2001

845 water bottle crates, PVC, wood, metal

216½ × 216½ × 177⅛ in. (549.9 × 549.5 × 450.1 cm)

Olafur Eliasson

Spiral Tunnel
2001
Stainless steel and lava rock, site specific
109⅛ × 720 × 150 in. (277.4 × 1,828.8 × 381 cm)

Unidentified Artist (Nigeria)

Mbembe Figural Post
From the Cross River Region, Nigeria
Wood

Wang Jin
Installation People's Republic of China, Passport No. 125109
2004
Eight sculpted stones
Dimensions variable

Cekis
Rosario
2011
Acrylic paint and aerosol on a wooden wall
110 × 10 ft. (33.5 × 3 m)

Artist Index

Acknowledgments

The origin of this publication dates back several years to a conversation among friends. Inspired by his first visit to ArtBarn, Steven Cornwell proposed creating a book that would document the extraordinary collection and celebrate the collector, Jerome Stern. The foundation that bears his name gratefully acknowledges Steven for his concept and subsequent contributions to the book as art director and cover designer, and his team member Anthony Nelson for book development. The Foundation's thanks go as well to Marcia E. Vetrocq for serving as project manager and editor. Thanks are also due to Christopher Burke Studios for photography of the artwork and the ArtBarn itself.

Work was suspended for a long period. Keith Fox reanimated the project and pointed the way to its eventual publication. We deeply appreciate his help. The Foundation thanks Holly LaDue, Jenny Mutch, Michael Vagnetti, Annalaura Palma, and everyone at Phaidon and Monacelli for bringing the book to fruition, and credits Shawn Hazen for the book's elegant design. The three authors—Christopher Phillips, Lisa Phillips, and Walter Robinson—provided insightful essays that contextualize the works and speak not only to the art and the ArtBarn, but also to the personal connections that made this collection so strong.

Finally, we dedicate this book with love and pride to the memory of the man, the collector, the legend, the inspiration to all of us, our rock and our glue: Jerry, Jerome, Dad, Grandpa.

Image Credits

Phaidon Press Limited
2 Cooperage Yard
London E15 2QR

Monacelli
A Phaidon Company
111 Broadway
New York, NY 10006

Phaidon SARL
55, rue Traversière
75012 Paris

phaidon.com/monacelli

First published 2025
© 2025 The Jerome L. Stern Family Foundation

ISBN 978-1-58093-686-6

Library of Congress Control Number: 2025907231

Every reasonable effort has been made to supply complete
and correct credits; errors or omissions will be corrected in
subsequent editions.

Editor: Jenny Mutch
Production: Michael Vagnetti
Design: Shawn Hazen

Printed in China